CAMRA'S **London**
Pub Walks

CAMRA'S **London**

Pub Walks

BOB STEEL

Published by the Campaign for Real Ale
230 Hatfield Road
St Albans
Hertfordshire AL1 4LW

www.camra.org.uk/books

ISBN-10 1-85249-216-3
ISBN-13 978-1-85249-216-8

A CIP catalogue record for this book is available from the British Library

Printed and bound in the United Kingdom at
the University Press, Cambridge

Head of Publications: Joanna Copestick
Editor: Adrian Tierney-Jones
Editorial Assistance: Debbie Williams; Emma Lloyd
Design/typography: Dale Tomlinson (and FB Amplitude)
Photographs: Bob Steel
Additional photographs: George Gimber *(pp. 123, 124 and 126)*
Maps: John Macklin
Marketing Manager: Georgina Rudman

ACKNOWLEDGEMENTS
The author would like to thank all those who
have helped in the preparation of this guide – in
particular, Jane Jephcote and Geoff Brandwood
for proof reading and countless suggestions for
improvement and corrections. Thanks also to
branches of the Campaign for Real Ale who
have reviewed the routes and suggested
improvements; in particular Geoff Strawbridge
for his meticulous scrutiny.

Of course, I alone take full responsibility for
the final product and any shortcomings therein.

Contents

Walk Locations

Numbers represent the approximate centre of each walk

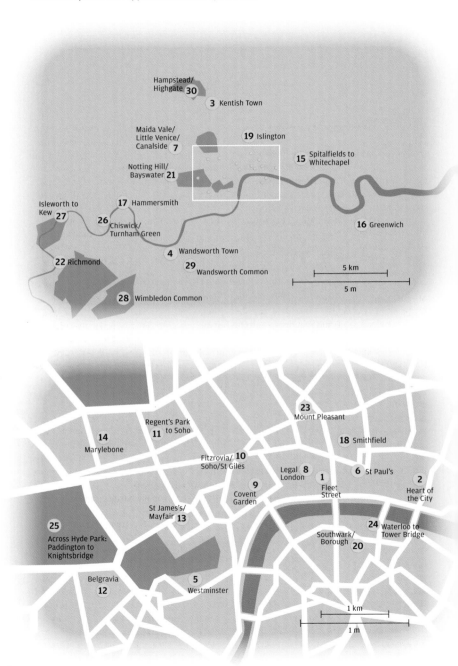

Hampstead/Highgate **30**

3 Kentish Town

Maida Vale/Little Venice/Canalside **7**

19 Islington

15 Spitalfields to Whitechapel

Notting Hill/Bayswater **21**

17 Hammersmith

Isleworth to Kew **27**

26 Chiswick/Turnham Green

16 Greenwich

4 Wandsworth Town

22 Richmond

29 Wandsworth Common

5 km

5 m

28 Wimbledon Common

23 Mount Pleasant

Regent's Park to Soho **11**

14 Marylebone

18 Smithfield

Fitzrovia/Soho/St Giles **10**

Legal London **8**

1

6 St Paul's

9 Covent Garden

Fleet Street

2 Heart of the City

St James's/Mayfair **13**

24 Waterloo to Tower Bridge

25
Across Hyde Park: Paddington to Knightsbridge

Southwark/Borough **20**

Belgravia **12**

5 Westminster

1 km

1 m

Introduction

Welcome to the Campaign for Real Ale's
London Pub Walks book. CAMRA was founded in 1971 and has become the most successful democratic consumer group in the United Kingdom with over 70,000 members. CAMRA's main aim has always been to safeguard traditional British beer, but as society has evolved so has the Campaign; and recently, both CAMRA and the discerning drinker have become increasingly concerned with the pubs in which we drink. In the last couple of years, this concern has borne fruit with the publication of CAMRA's *National Inventory* of significant pub interiors in 2003, followed by the first of the *Regional Inventories* for the London region (2004) and East Anglia (2005). *London Pub Walks* aims to showcase both of these issues, enabling you to undertake some real ale trails in the capital whilst visiting some of the best pub interiors left in London. So you don't have to be a real ale drinker to enjoy this book. The other thing we hope to achieve is to put the pubs in a spatial context. Plenty of books have been published about London pubs, often claiming to be about 'historic' pubs, although many of these have little authenticity left. Few London pub guides take you from one pub to the next, nor can claim the pedigree of and expertise from a ten-year project with English Heritage, when it comes to researching pub interiors.

Most of these trails take you to about 5 or 6 pubs, although there are links to adjacent trails if you have the stamina. Where possible we start and end at an Underground station, or failing that a National Rail station. Visitors to London will find the public transport system pretty good, despite its detractors. If you are a visitor to London, consider buying a Travelcard at the start of the day – if you

are making more than a couple of journeys by public transport it will be cost effective.

The trails are broadly arranged so that the shorter ones are towards the front – if the walking between pubs is just a necessary evil before the next drink, start with some of these. We have also included some routes where more walking is required, either because the pubs are further apart; or in a couple of cases, where there are green areas to enjoy, like Wimbledon Common. You will find these towards the back. For those who want a longer trail, there are links provided to enable you to switch from one trail to another in the central London area. Total walking distances are given in the information box at the beginning of each walk. The length of time that it takes to cover this distance is, of course, dependent upon how long you choose to spend in each pub and whether you take in any of the nearby attractions in a given area.

The trails are also organised so that you can start them in the morning, which if you are able to, is a great time to do them. There is something about being at the first pub as the bolts slide across at 11am that is almost guaranteed to give the day a good send off. The first pub on each trail opens at 11 am or earlier at the time of writing.

Many of the pubs in this book have also been featured in the *Good Beer Guide*, CAMRA's flagship best-selling annual guide book, whilst those of historic or architectural interest are listed in the CAMRA National or London Regional Inventory (see above and page 147). Remember though that pubs do change – landlords come and go, as do good and poor staff. We cannot guarantee that every pint you drink will be top quality every time. Please remember too that the range of beer in a particular pub may change – so take the notes about beers on offer at any pub as indicative rather than definitive. Those readers who are unfamiliar with the range of beers available in Britain should read the section on beer styles at the back of this book.

Food of course is now widely available in pubs; and the great majority of pubs in this book offer at least snacks and sandwiches. We have not religiously included food information for each pub. If you want to eat whilst on one of these trails, you should have no trouble, unless you decide to go at a very busy time or late in the evening.

As this book was being prepared, many pubs were applying for extended opening hours whilst renewing their licences. I have not attempted to indicate this here, but the times given were correct as of Summer 2005. As a rule the main changes to opening hours may be that several pubs will open an extra hour, or thirty minutes longer at weekends; probably not the best time to appreciate these trails anyway if you want to get the most from them.

Information on disabled access, and whether featured pubs allow children and dogs has not been included here. Pubs frequently revise their admissions policy, and although it is desirable for all licensed premises to have suitable access for disabled people, this is unfortunately not always the case. If you do have any special requirements please phone the establishments that you are planning to visit in advance. Telephone numbers have been provided in the pub information box at the end of each walk.

We have also rated each route according to the range of beers you are likely to find on each trail. Together with the pub architecture ratings they are a guide to what to expect.

Beer range on the trail as a whole:

- ★ Limited
- ★★ Good
- ★★★ Exceptional

Pub Architecture on the trail as a whole

- ★ Unexciting
- ★★ Good to very good
- ★★★ Outstanding

It's also important to bear in mind that many London pubs do not open at weekends, or have restricted hours. Broadly speaking, those in the City, towards the east of the central area, are more likely to be closed at weekends, but most of those in the West End will be open. Check the times on each entry, which were correct when going to press, but are subject to alteration.

Another thing to remember is that London pubs do get busy – in the City at lunchtimes, after work and in the West End of an evening. Not everyone is able to go at quieter times, but I think a great time to enjoy pubs is in the morning soon after they open, particularly if you want to appreciate the architecture.

If you are not a native of London, you may be put out at the prices. You have our sympathy as drinks prices in London are among the highest in the country. Be thankful that, having invested wisely in this book, you ought not to find yourself wasting your cash in inferior establishments.

Finally I have avoided the term 'pub crawl' in this book for good reason: good beer, and good buildings, are to be enjoyed at a sensible pace. Drink responsibly and enjoy the trails.

RWS
Carshalton, 2005

WALK 1 **Fleet Street**

WALK INFORMATION
Number of pubs: 5
Distance: 3/8 mile (0.6 km)
Key attractions:
Museum of London,
Dr Johnson's House,
St Bride's Church,
Temple Church.
Beer range: ★★
Pub architecture: ★★★
Links: to walk 8

This is the shortest walk in the book, but one rich in pubs with fine interiors. The route meanders from Blackfriars, through Ludgate Circus to Fleet Street, once the heart of London's printing and newspaper industry. This remains one of London's great streets, lined with a variety of fascinating buildings and pubs. No fewer than four of the pubs here appear on CAMRA's *London Regional Inventory* of historic pub interiors.

Start at Blackfriars and cross via the subway, exit 1, to the **Black Friar** 1. This also appears on the St Paul's walk, but I make no apologies for including this amazing pub twice. There isn't another quite like it! Grade II listed and jammed against the railway line, this narrow wedge-shaped pub was built circa 1875 on the site of a thirteenth-century Dominican Priory. This religious heritage gave the area its name and was the inspiration for the pub's design. The outside is very impressive, but it is the interior, dating from an Art Nouveau refit in 1905, that makes this pub so remarkable. The artists, including Royal Academy sculptor Henry Poole, used high quality materials such as marble and alabaster, while adorning the pub with the imaginary antics of the local Dominican friars. Look for the witty captions like 'Don't advertise, tell a gossip!' The intimate snug, dating from 1917, is especially notable. The main bar would originally have been partitioned with screens, but these have now gone. A plaque outside reminds us that some 30 years ago, the Black Friar nearly followed thousands of other fine pubs into oblivion, but was saved following a spirited campaign led by former poet laureate John Betjeman.

The exterior of the wedge-shaped **Black Friar**

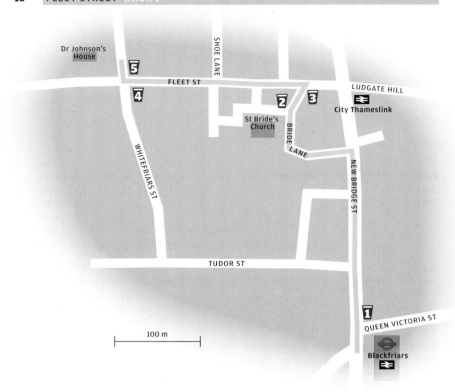

The Black Friar is a rare exception in an era of pub building when austerity was replacing the glamour and confidence of the late Victorian period and maybe that's why we have little else like it. This great pub is best enjoyed in the quiet period soon after opening time, and has a good range of draught beers from breweries such as Fuller's and Timothy Taylor.

Having enjoyed the Black Friar, walk up New Bridge Street past the new *El Vino's* and cross the road by the first set of lights. As you dodge the traffic note that you are now walking more or less over the old bed of the River Fleet which ran down through Ludgate Circus before being culverted in the eighteenth century. Turn left up Bridewell Place, a narrow street which gives way into a passage on the right. Here, the **Old Bell 2** sits on a corner opposite the imposing St Bride's church, which traditionally had close connections with journalists and printers. The church has the highest Wren steeple in London and was apparently the inspiration for the traditionally tiered

wedding cake. The spire was built in 1701-3 and withstood the Second World War Blitz although the rest of the church was destroyed in December 1940 and later rebuilt. The Old Bell was reputedly constructed to refresh the builders at work on the church. Despite alterations, it still has an atmospheric interior with plenty of wood and glass, and there is a striking floor mosaic in the entrance to the back door. Beers usually found here are from Timothy Taylor and Adnams.

The next pub is the **Punch Tavern 3**, approximately 15 yards to the right of the Old Bell. Originally called the *Crown and Sugarloaf*, it was on these premises in 1841 that *Punch* magazine was supposedly conceived. Staff of this satirical magazine met here for 150 years until it folded in 1992. Despite a rebuild in the mid 1890s, recent upheavals that have seen the pub divided in two, and a new *Crown and Sugarloaf* that has opened just around the corner, the Tavern retains some fine early features.

Note especially the splendid tiled entrance corridor with mosaic floor, presided over by paintings of Mr and Mrs Punch. Inside, there are two fine skylights and a nicely proportioned bar back boasting some rich etched glass. Geologists in particular will appreciate the bar top in pink marble and the attractive fireplace. The pub is now aimed at affluent city workers, with prices to match, and has an interesting food buffet. Beerwise, Timothy Taylor Landlord is the most regular ale on tap.

Now, walk back up Fleet Street to the west and while passing the Old Bell again, look out on the opposite side of the road for two of the finest monuments to the long-gone days of Fleet Street's newspaper culture. Number 135, the old *Daily Telegraph* building, was a very bold building for such a conservative newspaper, but was architecturally outflanked shortly afterwards by the glass curtain wall of the old *Daily Express* HQ just to the east, nicknamed the 'Black Lubyanka' by *Private Eye*. Our next pub, which is so overshadowed

by modern office blocks that it is easy to miss, is less than five minutes walk away. The **Tipperary** 4 claims to be the earliest Irish pub in London, a boast backed by the words on its exterior board that it was acquired and refitted by J G Mooney & Co of Dublin in 1895. The well-worn remains of the Mooney name appears on a slate at the entrance and shamrocks are found in the mosaic flooring. Starting life as the *Boar's Head*, the pub was renamed the Tipperary in 1918 to commemorate the Great War song. The ground floor bar is a long narrow room with wood panelling, inset mirrors and an imposing bar back. It is now owned by Greene King and real ales sold include their IPA.

Fleet Street used to run more or less along the Thames' shore, and the area retains many of the alleys and courtyards typical of medieval cities. It is in one of these that our next pub is found, with the sign visible across the street to the right on leaving the Tipperary. To reach the **Olde Cheshire Cheese** 5 in one piece, use the crossing and head right for a few yards to an alley with the distinctive name of Wine Office Court. [LINK] Here stands the atmospheric entrance to possibly London's best-known tourist attraction pub, an important survivor in the social history of the urban tavern, with its exterior pendant lantern giving the date of 1667, the year after the Great Fire. Inside, the original pub retains a domestic-style layout that is very rare in London pubs. Two rooms lead off the entrance corridor, conjuring up a sense of homeliness with their large fireplaces, while the vintage panelling is possibly the oldest of any London pub. It's easy to imagine the right-hand room without its Victorian bar counter, a reminder of a time when bar counters did not exist and drinks were brought to customers at their table in jugs or pitchers from the cellar. The Cheese stems from the tavern rather than the alehouse tradition, as it sold mainly wine and food and thereby catered for the upper and middle classes. The rear left-hand room continues in that tradition, with a long history of use as a dining room, going back at least to the days of Dr Johnson who was reputedly a patron here. In the dining room, hangs a Reynolds portrait of the sturdy lexicographer with the following inscription beneath:

> 'The Favourite Seat of Dr. Johnson…
> born 18th Septr, 1709. Died 13th Decr, 1784.
> In him a noble understanding and a
> masterly intellect were united with
> grand independence of character and
> unfailing goodness of heart, which won
> him the admiration of his own age,
> and remain as recommendations to the
> reverence of posterity. "No, Sir! There is
> nothing which has yet been contrived
> by man by which so much happiness
> has been produced as by a good tavern."'

Perhaps the best of the many poems penned in praise of this venerable house is the *Ballade* written by John Davidson (1857-1909) the Scottish poet, one stanza of which reads:

> *I know a house of antique ease*
> *Within the smoky city's pale,*
> *A spot wherein the spirit sees*
> *Old London through a thinner veil.*
> *The modern world so stiff and stale,*
> *You leave behind you when you please,*
> *For long clay pipes and great old ale*
> *And beefsteaks in the 'Cheshire Cheese'.*

The Cheese also has cellar rooms and an upstairs eatery but the two ground floor rooms are the kernel of the old tavern. Other curios are the old fly screens with 'OCC' inscribed on them, and above the doorway to the bar room there is an old warning: 'Gentlemen only served in this bar'.

Beyond the staircase, a 1991 extension has significantly increased the area of the pub; a good thing, for it gets very busy.

Fireplace in the **Olde Cheshire Cheese** and *(below)* the sign outs

The best time to visit is soon after opening time when you can appreciate the wonderful panelling and glazing unimpeded. The Cheese is owned by Sam Smith of Tadcaster, so expect their OBB on handpump.

Return to Fleet Street where the nearest Underground station is Blackfriars. Buses to the West End can be found across the road.

LINK Walk 8, **Legal London** (*page 37*). From the Olde Cheshire Cheese walk 250 yards west past St Dunstan's church to the *Old Bank of England* and the start of the walk.

PUB INFORMATION for walk 1 **Fleet Street**

1 Black Friar
174 Queen Victoria Street,
London EC4
020 7236 5474
11.30-11 Mon-Sat; 12-10.30 Sun
CAMRA Regional Inventory

2 Old Bell Tavern
95 Fleet Street, London EC4
020 7583 0216
11-11 Mon-Fri; 12-6 Sat;
Closed Sundays

3 Punch Tavern
99 Fleet Street, London EC4
020 7353 6658
11.30-11 Mon-Fri; 11.30-6 Sat;
12-3, 7-10.30 Sun
CAMRA Regional Inventory

4 Tipperary
66 Fleet Street, London EC4
020 7583 6470
11-11 Mon-Fri; 12-6 Sat-Sun
CAMRA Regional Inventory

5 Olde Cheshire Cheese
Wine Office Court,
145 Fleet Street, London EC4
020 7353 6170
11.30-11 Mon-Sat; 12-3 Sun
CAMRA Regional Inventory

WALK 2 **The Heart of the City**

WALK INFORMATION
Number of pubs: 7
Distance: ½ mile (0.8 km)
Key attractions:
The Royal Exchange,
Bank of England,
Leadenhall Market,
Museum of London.
Beer range ★★
Pub architecture: ★★★
Links: to walk 15

This compact seven-pub walk lies right in the heart of the City of London, close to many famous financial institutions like the Stock Market in Threadneedle Street, and the futuristic Lloyd's building to the east of Leadenhall Market. One important thing, note the *weekend closure of all the pubs*.

Start at Bank station, conveniently situated on both the Underground and Docklands Light Railway. Liverpool Street tube and national rail station are also only a 10-minute walk away. From Bank, walk east along Cornhill, maybe pausing first to admire the external charms of the Royal Exchange, rebuilt in the 1840s, before reaching our first pub, the **Counting House** ⓵. This sumptuous Grade II listed Fuller's house was formerly a branch of the National Westminster Bank and has only been a pub since 1997. It boasts a huge glass-domed ceiling and the old banking hall has been cleverly converted into a modern bar without detracting from the original features of the building. This excellent conversion led to the pub winning a City Heritage Award for being one of the finest examples of building refurbishment in the City, the first time that the City Heritage Award has been won by a public house. So, there are plenty of interesting features to admire, whilst sampling Fuller's beers.

Leave the Counting House via the rear door leading to St Peter's Alley, one of numerous little alleyways that have survived in the City. Turn right and go through an archway, then

Skylight at the **Counting House**

13

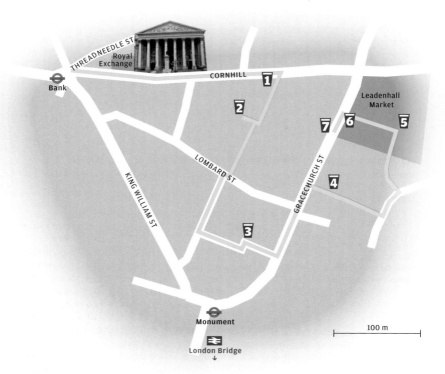

right again by some steps leading into a second alley by a small garden. Turn right, and there is our next pub, the distinctive **Jamaica Wine House** 2. If all these alleys are too much for you, simply exit the Counting House into Cornhill, turning left and then left again into St Michael's Alley. The Jamaica Wine House is an unusual pub with a long history dating back to 1652. It was built on the site of *Pasqua Rose's*, the world's first coffee house, where shares were traded before the Stock Exchange was set up 200 years ago. In 1674, the building became the *Jamaica Coffee House*, the vanguard of a coffee house tradition that numbered 3,000 in London by 1700. It is also known that this building was used for slave trade transactions from the 1740s until the abolition of this horrific trade in the early nineteenth century. Later, the Jamaica became the headquarters of a Victorian rum merchant. By 1869, it had become a wine house and the current building, in an unusual sandstone more akin to Glasgow than London,

Glasgow style in the City - the **Jamaica Wine House**

was constructed in 1885. The pub has had a serious makeover, although the interior on the ground floor retains three fine partitions and the original bar counter to give it sufficient character to earn a place on CAMRA's *London Regional Inventory* of pub interiors of historic interest. You'll probably be more impressed if you don't remember it before the refurbishment though. Look out also for the very fine external sign, and the interesting contrast in the ceiling styles of the different parts of the pub that might be evidence for later extensions to the building. The beer range varies, and includes Wells Bombardier and Greene King IPA.

Finding our next hostelry requires a little bit of navigation. Turn left out of the Jamaica into St Michael's Alley, walk past the small garden and then turn right into another small alley. Bear right again and you will be in George Yard. Cross into Clements Lane and turn left into Lombard Court, where lies the **Red Lion 3**, half-hidden in this quiet little alley. This is a handsome pub with plenty of dark woodwork and panelling, a nice though surely modern bar back and a marble-top bar counter. Typically, beers found here include Fuller's London Pride, Greene King IPA and a guest beer such as Wychwood. If it looks very busy try the spacious downstairs bar.

Come out of the Red Lion and Gracechurch Street is only a few yards away. Cross the road, then turn left and cross at the traffic lights, and you'll find a small alley, Ship Tavern Passage, just beyond Marks and Spencer's. You might expect a pub along here to be called the Ship Tavern, but in fact it's the **Swan 4**, another small wood-panelled pub, that is actually one of the smallest in the City, although there is another bar upstairs. Acquired by Fuller's Brewery in 1991, it's a popular place, with punters frequently spilling outside onto the pavement.

We are right on the edge of Leadenhall Market now, and taking the little alley beyond the Swan, turn left, then right and left again. With any luck you should now be within sight of our next pub, the very impressive **Lamb Tavern 5**. If all else fails, you could always simply walk up Gracechurch Street and turn in by the New Moon. The covered Leadenhall

The alley entrance to the **Swan**, one of the smallest pubs in the City

Market itself is a striking Victorian construction dating from 1881, although the site's history goes back to Roman times. Most of the pub trade in this area is geared to the affluent City crowd nowadays and this is also true of the Lamb, a magnificent building on three floors, rebuilt in its present style in 1881. After being a freehouse until 1985, The Lamb is now owned by Young's Brewery. The same family has managed it for 50 years, leading to a very good record of appearances in the *Good Beer Guide*. On a more esoteric note, the Lamb has been a film location for both *Brannigan* starring John Wayne and *Winds of War* starring Robert Mitchum. Beers come from the Young's range, and include their Bitter, Special and seasonal ales.

It is a mere hop, skip and jump to our next pub, the **New Moon 6**, an interesting and worthwhile port of call, though not quite as architecturally striking as the Lamb. This is another spacious building that can get very busy at lunchtimes and early evenings. Beers from a range of larger breweries are served here, and are normally in good condition. Details of the full range are displayed outside the pub.

If you're still in the mood for drinking, you will be pleased to note that across Gracechurch Street and slightly to your left, hidden behind the smart facade of yet another former bank, lies the **Crosse Keys 7**. This is an impressive Wetherspoon's pub that opened in 1999 in a former bank occupying some 8,000 square feet, massive even by

The splendid **Lamb Tavern** occupies a key site in the Leadenhall Market

Wetherspoon's standards. Built in 1912 for the Hong Kong & Shanghai Bank and named after the nearby *Crosse Key Inn* which was destroyed by the Great Fire of London in 1666, the building has a very high ceiling with glass-domed skylights, substantial marble pillars and a striking circular central bar in marble. One of the best parts of this Grade II listed building is the elegant wood-panelled room at the rear. To top it all, the range of real ales is likely to be one of the best in central London, provided that you can get served by the often hard-pressed staff, and includes Shepherd Neame Spitfire,

Greene King Abbot, Marston's Pedigree, Fuller's London Pride and guest beers.

From here, Monument underground station is five minutes' walk down Grace-church Street, or you can return to Bank simply by walking up the left hand side of the street and turning left into Cornhill. Alternatively, buses will take you to London Bridge and Liverpool Street underground and national rail stations.   [LINK]

LINK Walk 15, Spitalfields & Whitechapel (*page 71*). On foot or take a bus up Bishopsgate to Liverpool Street station and the start of the walk.

PUB INFORMATION for walk 2 **The Heart of the City**

1 Counting House
50 Cornhill, EC3
020 7283 7123
11–11 Mon–Fri
Closed Saturday & Sunday

2 Jamaica Wine House
St Michael's Alley, Cornhill, EC3
020 7929 6972
11–11 Mon–Fri
(may close earlier if quiet)
Closed Saturday & Sunday

3 Red Lion
8 Lombard Court, EC3
020 7929 2552
12–11 Mon–Fri
Closed Saturday & Sunday

4 Swan Ship Tavern Passage,
78 Gracechurch Street, EC3
020 7283 7712
11–9 Mon–Sat; Closed Sundays

5 Lamb Tavern
10–12 Leadenhall Market, EC3
020 7626 2454
11–9 Mon–Fri
Closed Saturday & Sunday

6 New Moon
88 Gracechurch Street, EC3
020 7626 3625
11–11 Mon–Fri
Closed Saturday & Sunday

7 Crosse Keys
7–12 Gracechurch Street, EC3
020 7623 4824
10am–11pm Mon–Fri; 10–7 Sat
Closed Sundays

WALK 3 **Kentish Town**

WALK INFORMATION

Number of pubs: 4
Distance: ¾ mile (1.2 km)
Key attractions:
Camden Lock Market,
Hampstead Heath.
Beer range: ★★
Pub architecture: ★★
Links: to walk 30

This is a short but rewarding ramble in a varied area between Kings Cross to the south and Highgate to the north. It's not an area for tourist sights, but although being part of the residential inner suburbs it's easily accessible by train, and nearby are the contrasting attractions of Hampstead Heath and Camden Town. It's also had more than its fair share of pub losses, many having been turned into residential use.

🏃 **Start at Kentish Town station**, which is sited on both the Thameslink and Northern Line underground. On emerging from the station, it's hard to miss your first pub, the **Assembly House 1**, as it dominates the road junction. It has very recently been refurbished in what appears to be the anticipation of imminent gentrification, if the first known sighting of the leather sofa in these parts is any guide. It's a big building, light and airy, and when it was constructed in 1896 it was typical of the late Victorian period. Inside there are several separate bars gathered around a central servery with a large saloon bar leading to an even bigger billiard room behind. Since then the pub has undergone a chequered history and much of its former character has been lost. Nonetheless, the skylight over the former billiard room remains and the surviving glass is some of the best you'll find anywhere. This was the work of local firm, William James, and is a joy to behold. Sadly most of the etched glass on the exterior windows has been lost, a probable mixture of brewery vandalism and past negligence by the local council. As for customers, expect all sorts in this landmark pub in a very mixed social

Wrought ironwork in the entrance to the **Assembly House**

Stunning etched glass and mirrors in the **Assembly House** (*above and below*)

area which is also close to a couple of big live music venues. The beer range is Greene King IPA and Abbot Ale.

After leaving the pub, walk eastwards along Leighton Road and take the first turning left into Leverton Street. Five minutes' walk up here brings us to one of Kentish Town's success stories in an area littered with the corpses of dead pubs. A vigorous local campaign in 2001–2 resulted in the listing of the **Pineapple** 7 and the defeat of an application to turn it into flats. It's easy to see why local people hold the place in such high regard. Inside there is a central servery surrounded by a horseshoe-shaped drinking area with a couple of small lobbies en route to a pleasant conservatory and garden at the rear. This all makes for a very relaxed ambience. Look out for the impressive mid-Victorian bar back with etched and gilded mirror work and two old Bass mirrors on the pub walls. Meanwhile, behind the unpretentious benches there is some old panelling. It is just the kind of pub in which one could

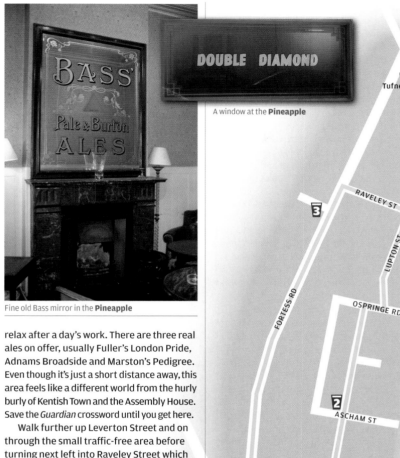

DOUBLE DIAMOND

A window at the **Pineapple**

Fine old Bass mirror in the **Pineapple**

relax after a day's work. There are three real ales on offer, usually Fuller's London Pride, Adnams Broadside and Marston's Pedigree. Even though it's just a short distance away, this area feels like a different world from the hurly burly of Kentish Town and the Assembly House. Save the *Guardian* crossword until you get here.

Walk further up Leverton Street and on through the small traffic-free area before turning next left into Raveley Street which leads us onto Fortess Road. Just down to the left on the opposite side is our next pub on this compact walk, the **Junction Tavern** 3. At first glance this looks like another casualty of the gastrophication of our pub heritage: loads of affluent thirty-somethings in the front room, tucking into a trendy menu backed with a massive wine list, give the impression that the whole place has been turned into a restaurant, but this is very much a pub of two halves. Enter through the side door and you come into an attractive and refurbished drinking area with lots of wood and, more importantly, the most interesting range of beers available in the area. Three hand pumps serve a rotating range, mainly from small microbreweries. Moreover, the pub holds its own beer festivals over the late May and August bank holidays. Look out for the elaborate mantelpiece over the fireplace and the interesting wooden bar counter under which even the old spittoon trough has survived. The backyard has been converted into a conservatory and a small but very attractive garden. Maybe this pub is a lesson for those who've completely destroyed the pub tradition in their haste to cash in on cash-rich bright young things. Even the word 'Tavern' in the name is a welcome survivor, since 'bar and restaurant' seems to be the designer favourite these days.

From here it's a short walk back down the hill to the centre of Kentish Town and, just on the right as we reach the traffic lights, is your last pub, the **Bull & Gate** 4, which is something of a local institution. A particularly ornate exterior entices one inside this mid-Victorian pub and, although you will normally only find Draught Bass available, you can consume it in attractive surroundings. This is another pub with an impressive bar back sporting cut glass. Note also the classical pillars and archway between the two main drinking areas. The screened-off room to the left is another ex-billiard room, now a venue for live music. This is a down-to-earth workaday boozer to finish with. Kentish Town station is just 100 yards away beyond the Assembly House (right upon exit).

LINK Walk 30, Hampstead & Highgate (*page 139*). Take an underground train from Kentish Town station to Hampstead via Camden or a 214 bus to Highgate.

Entrance and interior of the **Bull & Gate**

PUB INFORMATION for walk 3 **Kentish Town**

1 Assembly House
292-4 Kentish Town Road, NW5
020 7485 2031
12-11 Mon-Sat; 12-10.30 Sun
CAMRA Regional Inventory

2 Pineapple
51 Leverton Street, NW5
020 7485 6422
12-11 Mon-Sat; 12-10.30 Sun
CAMRA Regional Inventory

3 Junction Tavern
101 Fortess Road, NW5
020 7485 9400
12-11 Mon-Sat; 12-10.30 Sun

4 Bull & Gate
389 Kentish Town Road, NW5
020 7485 5358
12-11 Mon-Sat; 12-10.30 Sun
CAMRA Regional Inventory

WALK 4 **Wandsworth Town**

WALK INFORMATION
Number of pubs: 7
Distance: 1¼ miles (2 km)
Key attractions: Young's
Brewery, Mouth of River
Wandle, Wandsworth
Park & River Thames
walkway.
Beer range: ★
Pub architecture: ★★
Links: to walk 29

This trail takes you out of central London to the home of one of the capital's largest and oldest independent brewers, Young's. It's no surprise that you will be drinking their beers nearly everywhere on this trail, for the brewery has some fine pubs in its home territory. Wandsworth derives its name from the Wandle river, one of the few Thames tributaries in London to survive the indignity of being culverted. This is not the prettiest walk in the book, but the pubs more than compensate for being in the middle of a very urban landscape.

🏃 **Start at Wandsworth Town** national rail station, which is a 10-minute train trip from Waterloo; if you are coming from Victoria change at Clapham Junction. [LINK] Exit the station and straight opposite is your first pub of the day, the **Alma** 🚇. This is a prominent corner pub, named after the 1854 Crimean War battle. It has a handsome elevation with green glazed tiling below the traditional London yellow brickwork and no fewer than five doorways. However, the nasty modern windows and doors frankly look quite out of place. Inside, the place has been ruthlessly opened out and given a sort of café bar makeover; but it's light, spacious and airy and seems to work well, although more could be made of the surviving quality fittings. These include some decent woodwork, a period fireplace and, above all, some very fine back-painted mirrors. The mosaic roundels set in the wall bearing the name of the pub are an unusual and attractive feature. With Young's beers on tap and bar food it can get very busy, so the usual advice holds: try to get there early.

A beautiful back-painted mirror and mosaic in the **Alma**

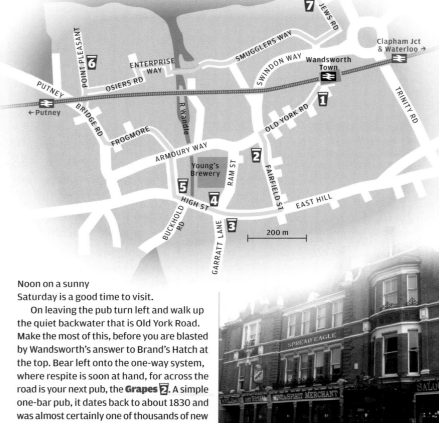

Noon on a sunny Saturday is a good time to visit.

On leaving the pub turn left and walk up the quiet backwater that is Old York Road. Make the most of this, before you are blasted by Wandsworth's answer to Brand's Hatch at the top. Bear left onto the one-way system, where respite is soon at hand, for across the road is your next pub, the **Grapes** 2. A simple one-bar pub, it dates back to about 1830 and was almost certainly one of thousands of new beer shops which came into existence as a result of the 1830 Beer Act. Young's have owned it since 1841, and at one time had a smithy on the premises. It has a nicely proportioned exterior with some terracotta work at ground floor level below the brickwork, and there is a pleasant garden which is a recommended retreat from the racetrack outside. Young's beers are available.

Follow the traffic round to the right on leaving the Grapes, taking you into the High Street. Before long, across the road, you will see the architectural highlight of this trail, the distinctive **Spread Eagle** 3. Just before entering the pub you will get a very good view of the brewery opposite. With the current building dating back to 1898, the golden age

Exterior and screen (*opposite*) in the **Spread Eagle**

of pub building, this is an impressive establishment, not least for its grand scale and sense of space. Mahogany joinery abounds. The bar back is large and adorned by mirrors, while large screens have survived, as has a wonderful skylight towards the rear. If the pub is quiet you may well feel dwarfed into insignificance by the scale of the place. Young's beers are available and there is food daily, except for Sundays.

Leaving the Spread Eagle, cross diagonally at the traffic lights to arrive at the Ram **Brewery Tap** 4, a fine well-proportioned building proudly occupying this corner site

Bread Eagle

and also offering brewery tours. Beer has been produced by Young's at the Ram Brewery since 1831, although it is claimed that brewing on this site goes back as far as 1581, making it the oldest site in Britain on which beer has been brewed continuously. The public bar of the Brewery Tap is now a shop selling Young's merchandise, but during the day the saloon bar is still open as a pub. With its decent 1930s interior, it is worth a visit. You can pop through into the shop too if the mood takes you. Be aware, however, of the pub's restricted hours: it's only open when the shop is.

From the Brewery Tap, head west along the High Street and on the next corner is yet another Young's house, the **King's Arms** 5. A cheerful, modernised interior lies behind the rather cold frontage; indeed this large pub has improved rapidly under new management who are giving it the 'tender loving care' that has been missing for some time. Comfortable sofas, chairs and bare floorboards are the order of the day in the large bar, and there is an adjacent room for overspill, though as yet the pub rarely gets

too busy. Food is a big player here too, but perhaps the biggest draw is the attractive and spacious garden stretching down to the River Wandle and offering another welcome respite from the sight and sound of the traffic. The brewery stands opposite, but with rumours that Young's may be about to relocate, one wonders for how long?

On exit from the King's Arms turn right down Wandsworth Plain. Cross over the northern limb of Armoury Way with great care and into Frogmore, some yards west of the *Crane* pub. This little road brings you out on to the Putney Bridge Road close to the Shepherd Neame-owned *Hop Pole*, which you may wish to try if only to vary the beer diet. Across the road by the rail bridge is the *Queen Adelaide*, recently re-opened after a refit but a past regular in the *Good Beer Guide*, so worth an exploratory visit if you have the time. No prizes for guessing the provenance of the beers! However, for our next pub, fork right into Point Pleasant at the bridge and walk down through a landscape of modern 'Legoland' flats and building sites to find, looking more like a beached whale than a moggie, the **Cat's Back** . This is a curious place, with a rather eclectic assembly of knick-knacks, but at the right time, especially by candlelight in the evenings, it's a pleasant and laidback place for a beer that isn't always Young's. In fact, the changing beer list here, which often has something from the likes of O'Hanlon's, Barnsley or Eccleshall, is one of the main attractions, despite the high prices.

The exterior of the **Cat's Back**

Whether it will survive the full-scale yuppification of this part of town is questionable. Many already say it isn't the place it was some years ago, but judge for yourself. Just beyond the pub is the river, with a privatised river walk to the right, but Wandsworth Park to the left might make a pleasant interlude if you need a siesta.

Otherwise, retrace your steps as far as Osiers Road on the left just before the railway bridge, and follow the Thames Path through a messy area into 'Enterprise Way' across the Wandle and into Smugglers Way. At the end of this road turn left into Marl Road, past the bus garage, left into Jews Row, and down towards the river and the **Ship** 7. This riverside pub has, like many others, been 'socially re-adjusted' to attract Wandsworth's bright young things, and become more food orientated. However, it is still atmospheric, whether you choose to sit inside, or enjoy the river terrace. There is also a relatively unspoilt little public bar on the landward side if you wish to escape the three-wheeled pushchairs and mobile phones. The beers are from Young's yet again. From the Ship it is but a short step back up the road to the station, which you will see as you walk up Jews Row. Cross the road with care. Frequent trains take you back to London, and of course if you miss one there is always the Alma...

LINK Walk 29, Wandsworth Common (page 133). Route starts from Clapham Junction, just one stop from Wandsworth Town by train.

PUB INFORMATION for walk 4 Wandsworth Town

1 Alma
499 Old York Road, SW18
020 8870 2537
12-11 Mon-Sat
12-10.30 Sun
CAMRA Regional Inventory

2 Grapes
39 Fairfield Street, SW18
020 8874 3414
11-11 Mon-Sat
12-10.30 Sun

3 Spread Eagle
71 High Street, SW18
020 8877 9809
11-11 Mon-Sat
12-10.30 Sun
CAMRA Regional Inventory

4 Brewery Tap
68 High Street, SW18
020 8870 2894
11-5 Mon-Fri
12-5 Sat
Closed Sundays

5 Kings Arms
96 High Street, SW18
020 8874 1428
11-11 Mon-Sat; 12-10.30 Sun

6 Cat's Back
86-88 Point Pleasant, SW18
020 8877 0818
11-11 Mon-Sat; 12-10.30 Sun

7 Ship
41 Jews Row, SW18
020 8870 9667
11-11 Mon-Sat; 12-10.30 Sun

WALK 5 **Westminster**

WALK INFORMATION
Number of pubs: 6
Distance: 1¼ miles (2 km)
Key attractions: Houses of
Parliament and Big Ben,
Westminster Abbey,
Cabinet War Rooms,
Buckingham Palace,
10 Downing Street,
St James's Park.
Beer range: ★★
Pub architecture: ★/★★
Links: to walks 8 and 13

This is one of two trails to start at Victoria Station, leading through backstreets on a sort of 'tourist bypass' down towards Parliament Square. The pubs are conveniently close to each other and there are plenty of interesting places to visit, including Westminster Abbey and the Houses of Parliament. On Sundays when the Cask & Glass is closed you can still start at Victoria but it's quicker to get the Underground to St James's Park and turn left up Petty France from the station to get to the Buckingham Arms.

From the front of Victoria Station, head for the ugly office blocks at about 45 degrees from the exit, which should take you to the right, across the busy Vauxhall Bridge Road. Then travel along the pavement, with the *Duke of York* across the road to your left, and under a canopy of concrete, glass and steel. If you are in the mood for a bit of sightseeing, Roman Catholic Westminster Cathedral is well recommended. The architecture of the cathedral certainly sets it apart from other London landmarks and it dates from the last years of the 19th century when London's most lavish pubs were being built. The towers and domes that you come across upon the piazza owe more to the Byzantine than the more normal Gothic or even Romanesque styles in which nearly all our other cathedrals are built. Inside, the cathedral is quite remarkable with some splendid marble work and mosaics. Of particular note too, are the world-renowned Stations of the Cross by the sculptor Eric Gill.

Just beyond the Cathedral Piazza, Palace Street leaves Victoria Street on the other side

of the road. Take this road and very soon you will reach the first pub of the walk, the **Cask & Glass** 🍺. Apart from being a Shepherd Neame house, two noteworthy things about this little pub are its compactness, which makes it one of London's smallest pubs, and the very fine floral displays that have long adorned the exterior. Also note the print-covered wood-panelled walls. If you can get

The attractive little **Cask & Glass**

here outside the busy lunch and after-work periods, it's a surprisingly quiet little place so close to Victoria Station. Bar food is available at lunchtimes but the pub is closed on Sundays.

Now take Wilfred Street, to the left upon exit, and at the end of the street turn right and then first left into Petty France. This oddly named street was formerly the more prosaic York Street but renamed after the French wool merchants who moved in during the seventeenth century. The passport office used to be here, but more importantly the excellent Grade II-listed **Buckingham Arms** 2 still is. Originally a shop, it became a pub in the 1840s and inside, a long, mirrored bar leads to a corridor drinking area at the rear. The Young's beer here is always on good form and the pub has an enviable record of continuous inclusion in every edition of the *Good Beer Guide*.

Just along the road from the Buckingham is the *Adam & Eve*, which you may wish to pop into if it's not too busy; it's closed at weekends though. With a spacious opened-out drinking area and up to five cask ales on at any one time it's a pleasant enough place if you can get a seat. There are still four pubs to visit, however, so maybe you will want to pace yourself and work up a thirst by continuing all of about 250 yards, past the underground station and on into what becomes Tothill Street. [LINK 1] As the bulk of Westminster Abbey comes into view, you'll see the somewhat less imposing façade of the **Sanctuary House** 3 on a corner site. Since 1997 this has been a Fuller's hotel sitting atop a well-regarded pub serving their range of ales. The décor is traditional with polished wood floors, benches and bar stools, and bar meals are available most hours.

Continue down the street until it opens out into the space adjacent to the Abbey. You may wish to visit now or at the end of the route, although be aware that the queues to get in are often horrendous. For those not familiar with all these fancy buildings, the Gothic façade of the Houses of Parliament, more properly called the Palace of Westminster, is straight ahead. Sadly, the entire original Palace, apart from the impressive medieval Westminster Hall, burnt down in 1834. Big Ben or, more precisely, St Stephen's

clock tower (since Big Ben actually refers to the bell), will need no introduction.

Turn left into Storey's Gate, past another famous London building, the Methodist Central Hall, opposite the brash modern Queen Elizabeth II Conference Centre, and ahead you will see the **Westminster Arms** 4. This pub must be, after your next port of call, the nearest to the seat of government across the road so it's no surprise that it feels like a mature place to come and drink. It also doubles as a wine bar. There is a cellar restaurant but of more immediate concern is the good range of cask ales from a number of larger breweries such as Greene King. If the attractive dark-panelled interior is too busy and it's not raining, there are a couple of tables outside from which to admire the impressive built environment around you.

At the end of Storey's Gate, cross the road and turn right to follow Great George Street along to the Parliament Square traffic lights. Cross at the lights, keeping in the same direction towards Westminster Bridge with Big Ben towering above you on the opposite side. Meanwhile, keep a look out for the

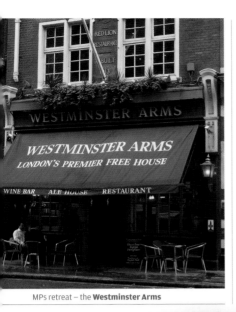

pendant lamp hanging outside our next stop on the first corner. **St Stephen's Tavern 5** is a pub that has come back from the dead, having been closed for over a decade. It was acquired by Hall & Woodhouse and reopened in 2003 after a very expensive refurbishment. Built in 1875, it takes its name from St Stephen's Tower across the road. The interior has been well restored with much to attract the eye; for example, the high bar back with some very fine mirrors, an ornate coffered ceiling with

MPs retreat – the **Westminster Arms**

Lamp outside **St Stephen's Tavern**

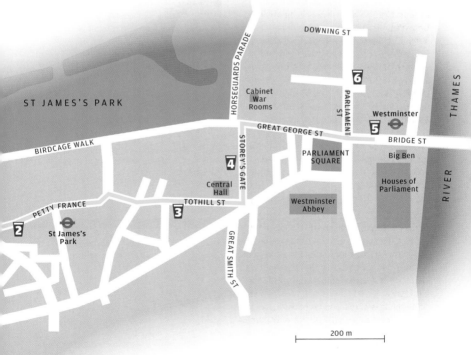

chandelier and a Victorian bar counter. Some of the window glass has survived too, particularly the very appealing 'Public Bar' door glass in the Bridge Street entrance. The exterior appearance is pretty stunning too as befits such a key location, with one of those wonderful big lamps hanging over each of the two main entrances. All sorts of the great, good and not so good have drunk here from the *other places* across the road, but these days you're far more likely to be sharing the bar with tourists. Up to four beers from the Hall & Woodhouse portfolio, including Tanglefoot, are on tap.

Your last port of call is a short stagger round the corner. Go back to the corner of Parliament Square and turn right into Parliament Street, soon to become Whitehall. The **Red Lion**  is a short distance along here and has the gravitas one would expect from a pub midway between No 10 and the House of Commons. This is yet another survivor from the turn-of-the-century 'golden age' and a lot of good-quality fittings remain from that time, among them a solid mahogany bar counter, plus some very pretty etched and cut glass and mirrors. The internal space is now a single long bar but clearly it was formerly divided. There is, however, a cellar bar if you can't find a seat, and an upstairs dining room. Beers once again come from the larger breweries.

Buses leave for Victoria Station from almost outside the pub, while Westminster underground on the District/Circle Line is around the corner just beyond St Stephen's Tavern. [**LINK 2**]

Victorian elegance at the **Red Lion**, Parliament Street

LINK 1 Walk 13, St James & Mayfair (*page 63*). Can be accessed after visiting the Buckingham Arms if you wish.

LINK 2 Walk 8, Legal London (*page 37*). One stop eastbound on the Underground will bring you to the start at Temple Station.

PUB INFORMATION for walk 5 **Westminster**

1 Cask & Glass
39 Palace Street, SW1
020 7834 7630
11-11 Mon-Fri; 12-8 Sat
Closed Sundays

2 Buckingham Arms
62 Petty France, SW1
020 7222 3386
11.30-11 Mon-Fri; 11-5.30 Sat
12-5.30 Sun

3 Sanctuary House
33 Tothill Street, SW1
020 7794 4044
11-11 Mon-Sat
12-10.30 Sun

4 Westminster Arms
9 Storey's Gate, SW1
020 7222 8520
11-11 Mon-Fri
12-5 (or 6) Sat-Sun

5 St Stephen's Tavern
10 Bridge Street, SW1
020 7925 2286
11-11 Mon-Sat; 12-10.30 Sun
CAMRA Regional Inventory

6 Red Lion
48 Parliament Street, SW1
020 7930 5826
11-11 Mon-Sat; 12-10.30 Sun
CAMRA Regional Inventory

WALK 6 **Around St Paul's**

WALK INFORMATION
Number of pubs: 6
Distance: 1¼ miles (2 km)
Key attractions: St Paul's Cathedral, Museum of London, Old Bailey, Temple Bar Monument, St Magnus the Martyr Church.
Beer range: ★★
Pub architecture: ★★
Links: to walks 2 and 18

This is a walk for during the week, since nearly all the pubs involved are closed at weekends. A pity, since this is an enjoyable stroll around and about the precincts of St Paul's Cathedral in a broadly linear route from Blackfriars to Cannon Street, passing through the small streets south of Ludgate Hill and past the Old Bailey.

Start at Blackfriars station, on National Rail and the Underground. Cross the road by the subway, following Exit 1, which brings you out right by the **Black Friar 1**. This is one of London's, and indeed the world's most amazing pubs, and even though it already appears in the Fleet Street walk this pub is so impressive that it can't be missed on this perambulation. *(See page 9 for Fleet Street.)*

After leaving the Black Friar, turn left under the rail bridge and left again up Black Friars Lane, taking a right into Playhouse Yard which becomes Ireland Yard ahead. At the end of this narrow passageway you'll find our next pub, the **Cockpit 2**. The dark exterior looks very seductive, but sadly the interior is a bit of an anticlimax although it is still an unusual shape at different levels. The story behind the name apparently comes from the time when cockfighting was popular here, until it was outlawed early in Queen Victoria's reign. The current interior is a curious quasi-medieval style complete with mini minstrel's gallery and dates back to a 1890s remodelling. Beers are from Courage.

Leave the Cockpit and take the narrow lane, Burgon Street, northwards, crossing Carter Lane into Creed Lane to emerge on Ludgate Hill with a dramatic view of St Paul's Cathedral to your right. Here, cross the road and turn left downhill towards Ludgate Circus, where the old Fleet river ran down to the Thames, hence the clearly outlined valley shape of the topography. Turn right up Old Bailey, the name recalling that this was the outer wall of the old City of London. Nowadays it's a gloomy street apart from the impressive Central Criminal Court at the northern end. Cross the road to get the best view of the gilded statue of Justice with her sword and scales. Until 1902, this was the site of the infamous Newgate prison.

Wonderful artwork in the **Black Friar**

Time for another stop, and across the road on a prominent corner stands the Grade II-listed **Viaduct Tavern** 3. Although remodelled at the turn of the century, the pub dates back to about 1870, taking its name from the nearby Holborn Viaduct opened in 1869. The four doorways suggest a once typically divided Victorian pub, although predictably the partitions have gone. However, many of the other original features have survived, the most prominent being the three large Victorian paintings of Rubenesque maidens, each representing a facet of London life: agriculture, commerce, and the arts. The latter painting was either shot or, according to some stories, bayoneted by a drunken soldier in World War I, and still carries the wound. Nowadays, the paintings are glazed to prevent further damage to the canvas. Between each of the paintings is one of several cherubic face reliefs that are a feature throughout the pub. Look out for the cut and gilded glasswork, especially towards the rear of the pub, where a little publican's office, once common but now a rare survivor, can also be seen. The cellars of the Viaduct are former cells of Newgate prison. It's a pity that the modern counter gantry, 'hideously inappropriate' according to the *CAMRA London Regional Inventory*, obscures or compromises much of the best work in the pub. Beers come from the larger brewers including Fuller's.   [LINK 1]

Some excellent mirror work has survived at the **Viaduct Tave**

Leave the Viaduct east along Newgate and cross the road, taking the pedestrian alley beyond Warwick Street, opposite the remains of Christ Church, Greyfriars. This leads into Paternoster Square with the view of St Paul's opening up. Below lies the restored and re-sited Temple Bar, another Wren edifice, which once stood on the Strand at the entrance to the city. During the eighteenth century, it was used to display the heads of traitors on iron spikes atop the main arch. Seen as a traffic impediment, it was taken down in the late nineteenth century, to be re-erected and later fall into neglect at Theobald's Park in Cheshunt. A stone set into the pavement gives the official reopening date, 10th November 2004, and it looks well in its rather sanitised new surroundings, with its handsomely

cleaned Portland stone blending nicely with the cathedral behind. The latter has itself recently been cleaned up and of course is well worth a visit if time and thirst permit!

Walk left around the northern side of St Paul's Churchyard, continuing right down the busy, dismal and mercifully short New Change, and turn left into Watling Street, which many will recognize as the name of the old Roman road from Dover to Wroxeter. Despite this, it is unlikely to be on the route of the original Roman road that traversed the Thames via the first London Bridge. Nonetheless, our next pub on this narrow street, the **Olde Watling** 🄸, has some claims to antiquity. It's plausible that the pub was, as it boasts, built to satisfy workers on the cathedral, and was constructed with old ship's timbers. Certainly this one-bar pub has some stern timbers that look the part, although it is hardly unspoilt. It's a small place, with floorboards and windows all around, while high stools line a wide shelf below them. A small room leads off to the rear, which is usually set out for diners. Besides Adnams and Fuller's, it's a welcome outlet for Harvey's Sussex Bitter.

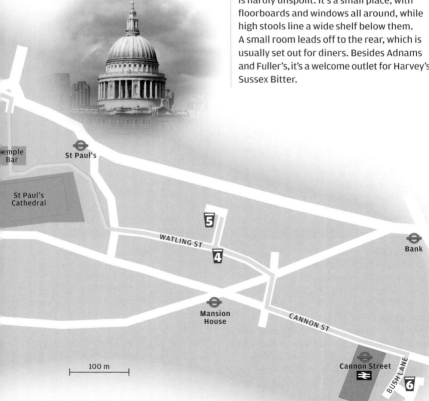

If you are still thirsty before our last leg of the trail, you may wish to try the **Williamson's Tavern** . This is very close by, in an atmospheric courtyard off Bow Lane (right opposite the Olde Watling), via some wrought iron gates. It's a 1930s pub with some character in its two interlinked rooms, and a decent range of real ales, with Fuller's London Pride and Adnams Bitter being regulars, alongside one or two rotating guest beers.

Now, continue down Watling Street past the interesting modern statue of The Cordwainer,

shoemakers to you and me: the weird name derives from Cordoba in Spain, which was highly regarded for its leather. Cross Queen Victoria Street, heading south down the short stretch of Queen Street to Cannon Street, then turn left and make your way towards the bold latticed office block adjacent to Cannon Street Station. Here, take the road on the right, Bush Lane, and your last port of call, the **Bell** , is on the left. It's a small pub on a road that once led down to the river. No doubt much altered, it has just one room with limited seating, but there is an inviting atmosphere. The well-kept beers are from Courage with some interesting guest beers, although like everywhere else around here it's not cheap! The gents' toilets are pleasantly old fashioned and pretty cosy if you encounter anyone else.

Public transport abounds when you come out of the Bell. If the Cannon Street stations, adjacent, are closed or otherwise of no use, walk to the right down Cannon Street to Monument underground, and buses across to London Bridge or north to Liverpool Street. [LINK 2]

Modern statue of The Cordwainer in Watling Street

LINK 1 Walk 18, Smithfield (*page 83*). Head north up Giltspur Street after leaving the Viaduct Tavern to locate the *Butcher's Hook and Cleaver* on the right hand side of the open space at the top of the street.

LINK 2 Walk 2, Heart of the City (*page 13*). Cross Cannon Street and head up St Swithin's Lane opposite to reach Bank in about 5 minutes, whence you can pick up the start of the walk.

PUB INFORMATION for walk 6 **Around St Paul's**

1 Black Friar
174 Queen Victoria Street, EC4
020 7236 5474
11.30–11 Mon–Sat
12–10.30 Sun

2 Cockpit
7 St Andrews Hill, EC4
020 7248 7315
11–11 Mon–Sat
(may close early Sat)
12–3; 7–10.30 Sun

3 Viaduct Tavern
126 Newgate Street, EC1
020 7600 1863
12–11 Mon–Fri
(may close early Mon, Tues)
Closed Saturday and Sunday

4 Olde Watling
29, Watling Street, EC4
020 7653 9971
11–11 Mon–Fri
Closed Saturday and Sunday

5 Williamson's Tavern
1 Groveland Court,
off Bow Lane, EC4
020 7248 5750
11–11 Mon–Fri
Closed Saturday and Sunday

6 Bell
29 Bush Lane, EC4
020 7626 7560
11–10 Mon–Fri
(*note early closing!*)
Closed Saturday and Sunday

WALK 7 Maida Vale, Little Venice and Canalside

WALK INFORMATION
Number of pubs: 5 (*1 closed*)
Distance: 1 mile (1.6 km)
Key attractions: Little Venice, Grand Union Canal, Regents Park
Beer range: ★★
Pub architecture: ★★★

This is a very worthwhile trail around some of London's most important pub interiors. Our walk takes us through the well-to-do streets of Maida Vale down to the well known Little Venice canal basin, finishing with a short walk along the Grand Union Canal. Although you can only visit four of the five pubs on this route, they are all the sort of places in which you might happily linger, finishing with a lazy afternoon sprawled in the sofas in the Bridge House, maybe.

Start at Maida Vale underground station, on the Bakerloo Line. Alternatively there are buses along the Edgware Road to the Hall Road junction. Leaving the station at Maida Vale, stroll southwards down Randolph Avenue and at the next junction the imposing splendour of our first pub, the **Warrington Hotel** 1, comes into view. Sadly the pub, dating from the mid-Victorian period but rebuilt around the turn of the last century, is no longer a hotel. On the other hand this is one of those pubs where the superlatives are entirely appropriate. Start at the palatial entrance porch round to the right, where there is a floor mosaic flanked by two stunning large lamps and the columns and walls are covered in glazed tiles. This is some of the best surviving ceramic work in a London pub. Inside, the huge saloon bar is dominated by a marble-topped, semi-circular bar counter, with a rich carved mahogany base. There is a lot of good Art Nouveau glasswork, although the paintings in a similar style on the canopy over the bar date from the 1960s and perpetuate the myth that the Warrington was once a brothel. Note also the well-proportioned

The palatial entrance to the **Warrington Hotel**

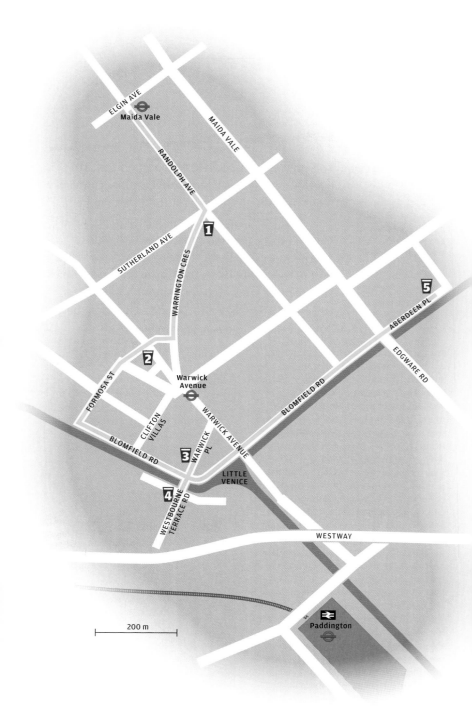

The horseshoe bar at the **Warrington**

staircase leading to an impressive upstairs landing and dining room with skylights and friezes. Here Thai food is served. The other room was once divided into three, as the evidence of screens and roof markings shows. All in all, the Warrington is a real *fin de siècle tour de force*. Beers come from the likes of Fuller's and Greene King plus guests.

Walk down Warrington Crescent with its fine terraces, turning first right into Formosa Street. On the next corner there is more to see in our second pub, the **Prince Alfred** 2. Even though this is another unique pub with a refit dating back to the golden age of London pub architecture at the end of the nineteenth century, the Alfred has sadly been subject to an unforgivable and inappropriate café-restaurant style makeover. This, coupled with creeping gentrification, has compromised its character so let's try to appreciate the good that remains. The once dowdy frontage with its splendid curved, etched windows has been restored to its former glory and, once through the entrance with its mosaic floor and tiled walls, we encounter the pub's unique feature – a series of separate compartments divided by half-height timber and glass screens which have low service doors leading from one compartment to another. A set of snob screens, looking

rather forlorn these days, survive in one compartment. There is plenty of good woodwork, notably the impressive, tall island bar back, which leads the eye up to an ornate ceiling. Let's hope the barbarians do not advance any further from the kitchen and do more damage to what remains. Beers come from the larger brewers, and having denigrated the architectural makeover of the eatery it's only fair to say that if you do eat here you are unlikely to be disappointed.

The exterior of the **Prince Alfred** is in the top league

Come out of the pub and continue along Formosa Street until it reaches the Grand Union Canal.

Pub architecture enthusiasts may wish to detour by taking a no. 187 or 414 bus up to the impressive *Chippenham* at the top end of Shirland Road. It has superb tilework although the pub as a whole looks rather sorry for itself at the moment and I cannot recommend the beer.

Walk along Blomfield Road with the Grand Union Canal on your right. This part of the Grand Junction Canal, as it was then known, was completed in 1801 with the later extension of the Regent's Canal. Take the second left into Warwick Place and you will come upon the attractive façade of the **Warwick Castle** 3 with its splendid iron bracket and large pendant lamp outside, overseen by a lousy new pub sign. Despite some modernisation, there are still many Victorian features. These include stained and etched glass, the bar counter, quite a lot of the panelling, friezes in the main bar and a lovely black and white marble fire surround in the second room. Fuller's London Pride is among the beers served here and food is available.

Walk back down to the canal and continue the few yards along to the bridge. An old lock keeper's cottage is visible below as you cross the bridge and, on the right hand side, the attractive Little Venice canal basin. Little Venice is the name given to the junction between the canal leading to Paddington Basin and the Regent's Canal. The canal here was opened in 1801 and forms a triangular basin with a little islet, hence the reference to Venice. It's a popular starting point for cruises along the most attractive part of the canal between here and Camden Town. Just immediately across the bridge is another little find and your last pub of the day if Crocker's is still closed. Despite its gastronomic pretensions, the **Bridge House** 4 is a pleasant and laid-back place, housed in an attractive neo-classical building. The seating is modern and the ambience agreeable. However, most importantly in a guide like this, the beers are interesting, with Timothy Taylor Landlord and Black Sheep Bitter served alongside a guest beer possibly from a micro brewery.

Walk along the canal, crossing back over the bridge first, on the Blomfield Road past Little Venice basin until you reach Edgware Road. This will take about five minutes. On your right, buses heading south will take you to Edgware Road underground station and towards Marble Arch and Victoria. However, it's worth a short detour straight across Edgware Road into Aberdeen Place where another five-minute walk will bring you to **Crocker's Folly** 5, originally the *Crown Hotel*, at number 24. Sadly closed at the time of writing and with an uncertain future, this is a Grade II* listed building with a late Victorian feast of marble, covering not only the counter but almost the entire bar. Moreover, the entrance saloon was, and hopefully will be again, one of London's finest pub rooms. It would be a fine finale to a walk of architectural superlatives. [LINK]

LINK Walk 14, **Marylebone** (*page 67*). A very short bus ride down the Edgware Road takes you there.

PUB INFORMATION for walk 7 **Maida Vale, Little Venice and Canalside**

1 Warrington Hotel
93 Warrington Crescent, W9
020 7286 2929
11–11 Mon–Sat
12–10.30 Sun
CAMRA National Inventory

2 Prince Alfred
5a Formosa Street, W9
020 7286 3287
12–11 Mon–Sat
12–10.30 Sun
CAMRA National Inventory

3 Warwick Castle
6 Warwick Place, W9
020 7603 3560
12–11 Mon–Sat; 12–10.30 Sun
CAMRA Regional Inventory

4 Bridge House
13 Westbourne Terrace Road, W2
020 7432 1361
12–11 Mon–Sat; 12–10.30 Sun

5 Crocker's Folly
24 Aberdeen Place, NW8
Currently closed

WALK 8 **Legal London**

WALK INFORMATION
Number of pubs: 5
Distance: 1 mile (1.6 km)
Key attractions:
Inns of Court,
Royal Courts of Justice,
Churches of St Dunstan's
and St Clement Danes.
Beer range: ★★★
Pub architecture: ★★/★★★
Links: to walks 1 and 10

This walk visits some of London's classic pubs as we meander on a linear route through the four Inns of Court, the collective name for the four 'honourable societies' in London that have the exclusive right of admission to the Bar. These societies are *Lincoln's Inn*, *Gray's Inn*, the *Inner Temple*, and the *Middle Temple*, and they date from before the fourteenth century. This is a walk best done in the week since some of the Inns of Court are closed to the public at weekends. The same is true for the pubs, particularly on Sundays.

Start at Temple underground station on the Embankment and exit into the gardens adjacent to the station. On the way you will pass several statues, notably that of Lady Somerset, a nineteenth century champion of temperance who would no doubt frown upon our purpose today! Exit and cross the road to the red phone box opposite and walk up Milford Lane to the steps ahead, taking us up into Essex Street. The steep rise is a reminder of a time when the area, now occupied by gardens, was once the marshy tidal flats of the river before the Embankment was built. Essex Street is named after the Earl of Essex, Robert Devereux, though the pub ahead has had its name changed from the *Essex Head* to the *Edgar Wallace*. However, if we turn right by this pub, the **Devereux** 1, our first stop on the next corner retains the association.

This place was formerly the *Grecian Coffee House*, opened in 1702, and frequented by Isaac Newton and Edmund Halley.

Robert Devereux's mansion, Essex House, inherited from his stepfather Robert Dudley, an intimate friend and advisor to Elizabeth I, also stood in the vicinity. Devereux himself, however, fell from grace and was beheaded in 1601 for high treason. The pub itself is intimate and pleasantly decorated with Arts and Crafts wallpaper, a gas-lit oak-panelled bar and carved wooden corbels. Courage beers and Old Speckled Hen are regulars and there is usually an interesting guest ale.

Go through the gates opposite into the precincts of the Middle Temple. The name of the Temple derives from the Knights Templar, a religious order of military monks formed in 1119 to protect pilgrims *en route* to the Holy Land. Their red cross on a white background can be seen in the grounds. The oldest and most interesting part of the Temple today is the church built by the Knights and consecrated in 1185. However, much of the Temple was destroyed in the Blitz and the majority of what we see today is a postwar reconstruction.

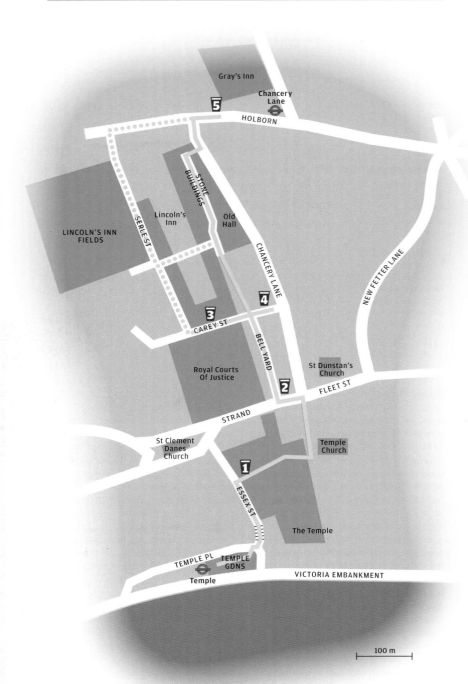

Gray's Inn

Chancery
Lane

5

HOLBORN

STONE
BUILDINGS

SERLE ST

Lincoln's
Inn

Old
Hall

LINCOLN'S INN
FIELDS

CHANCERY LANE

NEW FETTER LANE

4

3

CAREY ST

BELL YARD

Royal Courts
Of Justice

St Dunstan's
Church

2

FLEET ST

STRAND

St Clement
Danes
Church

Temple
Church

1

ESSEX ST

The Temple

TEMPLE PL   TEMPLE
GDNS

VICTORIA EMBANKMENT

Temple

100 m

Walk through the arch opposite, dated 1677, and through Pump Court arch to arrive at Temple Church. Turn north, keeping left of the church to exit on Fleet Street. If the Temple is closed, go back to the *Edgar Wallace* and turn right to arrive on the Strand, then turn right again. Before continuing the pub tour you may enjoy a short detour to view Prince Henry's Room, a fine Jacobean building pretty much above the exit from the Temple, with a splendid plasterwork ceiling in the wood-panelled first-floor room, and material connected with diarist Samuel Pepys. If there is time, wander across the street to the church of St Dunstan's-in-the-West with its distinctive 1830s octagonal tower and lantern. The clock tower adjacent is far older and was erected in thanksgiving for deliverance from the Great Fire of 1666. The splendid clock is presided over by Gog and Magog who strike the bell every hour, whilst close by, another survivor of the fire is the stone statue of Queen Elizabeth I, the oldest of that monarch still remaining in London, which probably dates from 1586.

Gog & Magog poised to strike at St Dunstan's Church

The imposing **Old Bank of England** 7 is across the road just left of the exit from the Temple. This impressive Grade I listed building has only been a pub since 1995 but was erected in 1886-8 as the Law Courts' branch of the Bank of England. It was designed in the Italianate style, popular at the time. Ironically, an historic pub, the *Cock*, was moved across Fleet Street to make way for the new bank; this still survives, but is not recommended. Fuller's has spent a small fortune restoring and decorating the Old Bank, and has also commissioned new paintings and murals. Large columns rise up to the high ornate plaster ceiling and from this hang three very large brass chandeliers. The central stillion itself almost reaches the ceiling. For a good view you can climb to a gallery where there is further seating. Along with the *Counting House* in Cornhill, this pub must rank as one of London's very best bank conversions, and you can enjoy the place with a glass from Fuller's excellent range of beers.   [LINK]

Leaving the Old Bank and taking Bell Yard, the alleyway immediately to the west of the building, walk up alongside the edge of the

Stunning decoration in the **Old Bank of England**

Royal Courts of Justice, the nation's main civil courts. This imposing Victorian Gothic building, designed by G E Street, is faced with Portland stone and was opened by Queen Victoria in 1882. At the top of Bell Yard turn left into Carey Street. Once home of the bankruptcy courts and through this once known colloquially as 'Queer Street' (although this archaic reference is now obscure), the street has had connections with many glitterati from Thomas More to David Bowie, who worked briefly at a printers here. But it is also home to one of London's classic pubs, the **Seven Stars** 3. Originally built at the end of Elizabeth's reign in 1602, it is one of the few buildings to have escaped the Great Fire in 1666, and recently, renovations revealed genuine 400-year-old timbers. However, the current timbered ground-floor frontage probably dates from the mid to late Victorian period. The exterior betrays the pub's expansion to the right. The etched and gilded glass in the doorways advertises 'General Counter' and 'Private Counter' but this small pub is now a single space. Inside you'll see some nice old mirrors and woodwork. The atmosphere owes much to the landlady, Roxy who, like her food, is the stuff of legend. Furthermore, like any pub worth its salt, there is a resident moggy. The beer is tasty too with Harvey's and Adnams as regulars, while Dark Star's Hophead made a welcome appearance recently.

Now, retrace your steps down to the eastern end of Carey Street and there is the **Knights Templar** 4, a Wetherspoon's bank conversion. It is not quite in the same league as the Old Bank in terms of adornment, although it is certainly pretty loud as far as the décor is concerned. It does, however, have a nice little non-smoking mezzanine and some very classy toilets as is often the case with JDW pubs. On the beer side of things, the usual Wetherspoon's choices alongside some interesting guest beers make it worth a visit, especially outside the busy times of lunchtimes and evenings.

If *Lincoln's Inn* is open, retrace your steps again towards the Seven Stars and, 100 yards before the pub turn right into the Inn at the New Square gate. If it is closed, continue to the corner of Serle Street and turn right.

The gate into the Inn from Serle Street is open longer on weekdays, so it will be possible to go in and look at the Inn if you wish. Note that the Inn is closed to the public at weekends. Continue up Serle Street, past Lincoln's Inn Fields on your left, to exit via a narrow alleyway into High Holborn, then turn right to join the route at the junction with Chancery Lane. Unlike the Temple, *Lincoln's Inn* miraculously escaped wartime destruction so retains its old buildings. The whole place is a haven of tranquillity, and is indubitably the most attractive of the four Inns. About 200 yards away, and opposite the main gate to the left, turn right then left via Old Square into Stone Buildings, with a Palladian Portland stone façade ahead. In this small courtyard, note the handsome Hogarth Chambers and the fifteenth century Old Hall and Lincoln's Inn chapel.

At the far end of Stone Buildings, exit via a small gate into Chancery Lane, an old London street commemorating the *Inns of Chancery*, now extinct lesser law societies and in effect preparatory colleges, dependent upon the Inns of Court. Turn left here, and cross High Holborn at the lights, whence the **Cittie of Yorke** 5 is a 100-yard stroll along to the right. Named after a pub that occupied a site across the road until the 1970s, this is the finest survivor of a pub style popular during the interwar years, which tried to evoke a return to an Olde Englande of medieval banqueting halls. Despite the apparent antiquity of the place, and numerous references to a Victorian pub by authors who should know better, the ground-floor pub dates back only as far as 1923, when it was rebuilt as a *Henekey's* wine bar. Enter via a corridor and to the left is a panelled mock-Tudor room. A cellar bar, which is a remnant of a much older building, is sometimes open and also worth a look. However, it is the rear room, built in the style of a great timber hall with a high-pitched roof, which is the jewel here. There is little like it in any English pub, with its arcade under clerestory windows, an array of small railway carriage-style booths and, above the servery, a walkway to serve the huge casks which at one time contained wine. Don't miss the fine old early

The incomparable **The Cittie of Yorke**

Clerestory and confessionals! The **Cittie of Yorke**

nineteenth-century triangular stove in the centre of the room, another unique fixture with an unusual flue that exits downwards. The pub is owned by Samuel Smith's of Tadcaster, so expect their Old Brewery Bitter. Good food is available most of the day from a modern servery at the near end of the room, but this is a pub to enjoy first and foremost for its architecture. [LINK 2]

The fourth of the Inns of Court, *Gray's Inn*, is conveniently located adjacent, with the entrance immediately east of the Cittie of Yorke. During opening hours it is worth a look, although after the delights of the *Lincoln's Inn* and the Cittie of Yorke it will be a bit of an anticlimax.

The nearest tube is Chancery Lane down Holborn to the east but buses run to many parts, including Liverpool Street and London Bridge; or to Waterloo and Oxford Circus on the opposite side of the road.

LINK 1 Walk 1, **Fleet Street** (*page 9*). A short walk east down Fleet Street from the Old Bank of England brings you to the Olde Cheshire Cheese from where one can do the trail in reverse.

LINK 2 Walk 10, **Centrepoint horseshoe** (*page 49*). From the Cittie of Yorke, walk or take a bus along High Holborn west to Holborn Station and just beyond is the Princess Louise.

PUB INFORMATION for walk 8 Legal London

1 Devereux
20 Devereux Court, WC2
020 7583 4562
11–11 Mon–Fri
Closed Saturday and Sunday

2 Old Bank of England
194 Fleet Street, EC4
020 7430 2255
11–11 Mon–Fri
Closed Saturday and Sunday

3 Seven Stars
53 Carey Street, WC2
020 7242 8521
11–11 Mon–Sat
Closed Sundays
CAMRA Regional Inventory

4 Knights Templar
95 Chancery Lane, WC2
020 7831 2660
10–11 Mon–Fri; 11–6/7 Sat
Closed Sundays

5 Cittie of Yorke
22 High Holborn, WC1
020 7242 7670
11–11 Mon–Sat
Closed Sundays
CAMRA National Inventory

WALK 9 A Circuit of Covent Garden

WALK INFORMATION
Number of pubs: 6
Distance: 1 mile (1.6 km)
Key attractions:
Covent Garden,
Royal Opera House,
London Transport Museum,
Trafalgar Square,
National Gallery.
Beer range: ★★/★★★
Pub architecture: ★★★
Links: to walk 8

The West End district of Covent Garden is one of London's success stories. In the 1970s, it was threatened with a dismal office-led redevelopment after the departure of the fruit and vegetable market, but a spirited campaign by local residents managed to fight off the developers. Our walk circumnavigates the old market hall, piazza and associated buildings, including the expanded Royal Opera House, Inigo Jones' St Paul's church and the London Transport Museum. If you are not a regular visitor to London you may well want to spend some time sightseeing in this interesting area and yet again this is a route to do, if you can, at quieter times!

Start at Charing Cross National Rail station or Embankment underground. In daylight hours, the nicest start to the trail is through the Victoria Embankment Gardens, at the foot of Villiers Street; otherwise simply aim for your first pub by walking east along the Strand, at the top of Villiers Street. The journey through the pleasant gardens will take you past the old Watergate which led out onto the Thames before the embankment was reclaimed. At the statue of Robert Raikes, the founder of the Sunday Schools movement, leave by the gate and straight ahead, up Carting Lane and the staircase, will be the welcoming sign of our first pub, the **Coal Hole** 🔟. With the name commemorating the coal-heavers of the Thames, this is part of Thomas Collcutt's Savoy complex but was opened in 1904 as the *New Strand Wine Lodge*. The name is still visible on the

front fascia. Here, Art Nouveau features mingle with elements of the 'Olde England' revival, which are even better exemplified in the *Cittie of Yorke* on the Legal London trail, route 8. There is a good deal of dark panelling, leaded windows and decoration. Under the beamed ceiling a plaster frieze depicts maidens picking grapes and there is a decorated fire surround towards the rear where the gallery is a converted office. The small basement snug is used as a wine bar. Beers usually available include Timothy Taylor Landlord and Fuller's London Pride.

From the Coal Hole make your way across the Strand and up Southampton Street opposite. Ahead lies the old Covent Garden market building dating from the 1830s and now a mecca of entertainment, shops and cafés. Take the left turn into Maiden Lane at the top of the short rise,

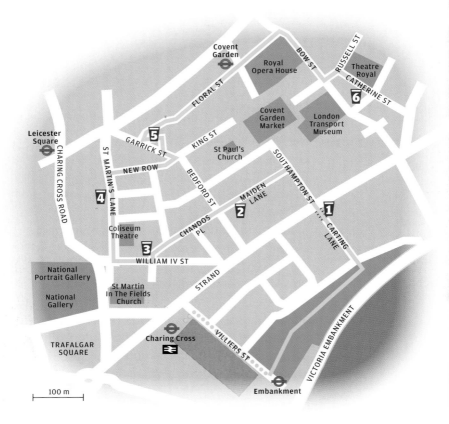

and walk along until you encounter the remarkable **Porterhouse** 2 on the left. This pub, owned by the Dublin company of the same name, won the CAMRA/English Heritage award for conversion to pub use in 2002. Here, you'll encounter a fascinating multi-level interior replete with wood and brasswork, and lots of nooks and crannies in a modern style. Most of the brews are served under pressure so they are not strictly real ales, aside from the TSB (Turner's Sticklebract Bitter). A guest real ale is also occasionally on offer. This is a pub to enjoy without the crowds.

Now continue further along Maiden Lane, and crossing over into Chandos Place, you can see two pub signs almost adjacent to

one other. The furthest one is the excellent **Harp** 3 and our next quarry. This small narrow pub, which has little that's Irish about it despite the name, has stained glass windows which open in good weather to allow a better view of the traffic snarl-ups outside. The interior has stools around the wall below a wide shelf, above which are a collection of paintings. An impressive array of pump clips hang all around the bar, where there are usually five well-kept ales on offer. These include Fuller's London Pride, Timothy Taylor Landlord and Black Sheep Bitter, plus two guests, one of which has often been a beer from Titanic. It's primarily a pub for drinking, although the award winning O'Hagan's sausages are available.

The award winning interior of the **Porterhouse**

If you have the time and the inclination, the *Marquis of Granby* is practically next door and is another pub well worth a visit. Sited on an odd triangular plot that comes to a very sharp point, it offers a good range of beers, with Caledonian Deuchars IPA a regular.

Continue beyond the Harp to the *Chandos* on the corner of St Martin's Lane, (you may wish to take a cultural detour to the numerous attractions around Trafalgar Square at this point, or at least admire the attractive steeple of St Martin-in-the-Fields church), then turn up to the right, past the rejuvenated Coliseum theatre, and very soon you will see the splendid exterior of the **Salisbury** across the street. From an architectural perspective there is little doubt that even on a trail like this the Salisbury is the highpoint, and it is pleasing to see the pride which the management take in the pub's heritage.

Exterior of the **Salisbury**

Rebuilt in 1892, and then called the *Salisbury Stores* (note the double 'S' in the etched windows), this building fully conveys the sense of glamour of the late Victorian pub and the interior is definitely one of the best in all London. The exterior is also pretty stunning and repays close inspection before venturing in. Inside, something of the divided-up plan survives with the small, screened snug on St Martin's Court. The original counter survives and you can mark the position of a now vanished partition by noting the change from wood to marble. The bar back is also very fine, as is some, though not all, of the glass. Perhaps the *tour de force* is the row of bronze Art Nouveau nymphs holding electric lamps. The beers come from familiar brewers, although Caledonian Deuchars IPA makes an occasional appearance. Food is available until mid evening.

Leaving the Salisbury, re-cross St Martin's Lane and head down New Row. However, rather than making for the Covent Garden market as it comes into view, start to bear left at the *Round-house* on the corner, at which point you will see another famous London pub at the end of a short lane across the street. This is the **Lamb & Flag** 🚩. The smart postwar red brick frontage conceals an ancient interior with origins in the late seventeenth century, with well-worn boards and panelling, and a lot of atmosphere to savour if you call at one of the few quiet times. The front space with the two doorways has been opened out in recent times. There was a small lounge to the left, hence the sign above pointing right to the public bar, but at the rear there is still an atmospheric room with a couple of old tables. This is one of the last free houses left in the area, and offers up to

The **Lamb & Flag**

six real ales, usually including those from Courage, Greene King, and Young's. Sandwiches and snacks can be had downstairs, whilst more substantial, good value meals are available in the Dryden Room upstairs.

Why Dryden? The poet John Dryden was beaten to within an inch of his life outside the Lamb in 1679 for writing uncomplimentary words about Charles II's mistress. This violence would become a regular feature of the pub's life as the years went on. In the early nineteenth century, the pub gained the nickname the 'Bucket of Blood' because of the bare-knuckled prizefights outside and in the rear room. In fact the whole area was a notorious slum in which fights were commonplace. Today the only fight you will be involved in is the one to get to the bar if you arrive at the wrong time. Back inside, don't miss the array of little brass plaques named for various customers, not all of them celebrities. Finally, those with a penchant for pub names will maybe recognise the flag as the red cross of the Knights Templar, carried on the Pascal Lamb of God.

Go through the narrow little alleyway alongside the pub (mind your head!) and into Floral Street. Turn right along this street dominated by top fashion names, until you hit James Street. This is the main pedestrian mall between Covent Garden underground station and the market, by the *Nag's Head* pub. Although the ale in this rare London McMullen's tied house is perfectly acceptable, the pub is nearly always crowded by virtue of its location and on that account I would avoid it. Instead, continue across by the Royal Opera House to reach Bow Street, where the Young's owned *Marquess of Anglesey* is to the right.

Then turn left and first right into Catherine Street and the famous Theatre Royal, which dates back to 1812. Just opposite is our last pub, the ornate-looking **Opera Tavern** 6. Rebuilt in 1879, it was the most elaborate work by the then well-known pub architect George Treacher. Two small bay windows project from the frontage. Inside, the pub is small, dominated by a fine wood and glass bar back while a tiled fireplace is also another survivor from the past. There is, however, an upstairs room for busier times and does the pub get busy! The pub advertises interval drinks for theatre-goers, which can be ordered in advance. The three beer engines offer a rotating selection of familiar but well-kept ales such as Fuller's, which you can sip while reading a framed cutting which recalls an incident in World War I when a German Zeppelin bomb fell hereabouts killing 38 people.

Public transport options upon leaving include Covent Garden underground, which you can reach by retracing your route to the *Nag's Head*, then turning right. If you are heading south, however, why not take the RV1 bus, which starts pretty well opposite here in Catherine Street and goes to Waterloo then on towards London Bridge. To get back to Charing Cross, simply walk down Catherine Street to the Aldwych and bear right down to the Strand. It is now a ten-minute walk or a short bus ride.   **[LINK]**

LINK Walk 8, **Legal London** (*page 37*). A short walk or bus ride (Nos. 11, 15 or 23) east around the Aldwych and beyond the law courts brings you to the Old Bank of England. A little further will take you to the end of the Fleet Street trail, walk 1, at the Olde Cheshire Cheese.

PUB INFORMATION for walk 9 **A Circuit of Covent Garden**

1 Coal Hole
91 Strand, WC2
020 7379 9883
11–11 Mon–Sat; 12–6 Sun
CAMRA Regional Inventory

2 Porterhouse
21–22 Maiden Lane, WC2
020 7379 7917
11–11 Mon–Sat (11.30 Fri & Sat)
12–10.30 Sun

3 Harp
47 Chandos Place, WC2
020 7836 0291
11–11 Mon–Sat
12–10.30 Sun

4 Salisbury
90 St Martin's Lane, WC2
020 7836 5863
11–11 Mon–Sat; 12–10.30 Sun
CAMRA National Inventory

5 Lamb & Flag
33 Rose Street, WC2
020 7497 9504
11–11 Mon–Sat; 12–10.30 Sun
CAMRA Regional Inventory

6 Opera Tavern
21 Catherine Street, WC2
020 7379 9832
11–11 Mon–Sat; 12–7 Sun

WALK 10 Centre Point Horseshoe: Fitzrovia, Soho & St Giles

Number of pubs: 8
Distance: 1½ mile (2.4 km)
Key attractions: Soho, Oxford Street, British Museum, St George's Church, St Giles Church, Bloomsbury Square.
Beer range: ★★/★★★
Pub architecture: ★★★
Links: to walk 9

This walk follows a broad arc around Centre Point, one of the earliest of London's tower blocks, and it is a real feast, not just for the good range of beers to be had but particularly for the pubs themselves. No fewer than three have a place on CAMRA's *National Inventory* of pub interiors and the rest all have plenty to look at. The walk can easily be shortened by omitting the first two stops and starting at Tottenham Court Road, practically adjacent to the Tottenham pub.

🏃 **Start at Goodge Street station** on the Northern Line and, on exit, turn left and left again into Tottenham Street. As the pub is on the first corner there is no real chance of working up a thirst here. The **Hope 1** is a fairly small local with one drinking area. It is smart but unpretentious, although the background music can be loud at the wrong time. Beers usually include Timothy Taylor's Landlord and food is served at lunchtimes only.

Turn left down Whitfield Street upon leaving the Hope, and second right into Goodge Street. Fitzrovia is an area which is still very well served with pubs, and you never have to walk far to find one. On the whole, the quality is pretty good too so some perfectly decent pubs such as the Young's-owned *One Tun* have been omitted. The *One Tun* can be found a little way along Goodge Street to the west and you may want to investigate it if you have the time especially since it is an ideal weekend alternative to the Newman Arms below. However, continuing on our stroll, just before the *One Tun* turn left down an alley to pass the

Duke of York pub and join Rathbone Street. The tiny **Newman Arms 2** on the right is something of an institution. Famous for its pies served in the small upstairs diner, the Newman is an attractive building inside and out although you may find it difficult to get a seat. Even without partaking of the pies however, it's an interesting place to visit. Fuller's London Pride is on tap.

Carry on down past the *Marquis of Granby* and turn right into Rathbone Place which brings you to the hurly burly of Oxford Street. Turn left towards the Centre Point tower. Once, there were about twenty pubs on Oxford Street, but now there's only one. The **Tottenham 3** was built in 1892 and, although it has lost some internal divisions, there is still much to enjoy in this pub. The interior is a long, narrow space, adorned with impressive tile and mirror work. Of particular note are the glazed paintings representing the seasons. Due to its location, it attracts mainly passing trade rather than regular punters. It can get busy, especially if there's a gig on at the Astoria over the road, so choose your time carefully. Beers available include Everards Tiger.

If we retrace our steps west along the crowded street and cross the road, the first turning on the left is Soho Street. Here we come upon the attractive Soho Square with its octagonal mock-Tudor shed which doubles as a ventilation shaft for the Underground. Soho is one of London's best known and most Bohemian districts, which has ridden a roller coaster ride from wealth to poverty and back again. At the far left-hand corner of the square Greek Street leads off south. Whisky enthusiasts may find the lure of *Milroy's* emporium at

No.3 too great to resist. A little further on, look for the alleyway on the left through to *Foyles* bookshop in Manette Street. We will be using this route later. The first turning beyond, on the right, is Bateman Street and this brings us to what is arguably Soho's best pub, the old **Dog and Duck 4**. Dating back to 1897, the splendid little pub has a fine interior adorned with good quality tile and mirror work. Look out for the yellow tiles with the two animals portrayed, under the large advertising mirrors. There remains a little semi-enclosed snug at the rear of the pub, although quite a bit of re-arranging

The exterior of the **Tottenham**

The distinctive exterior of the old **Dog and Duck**

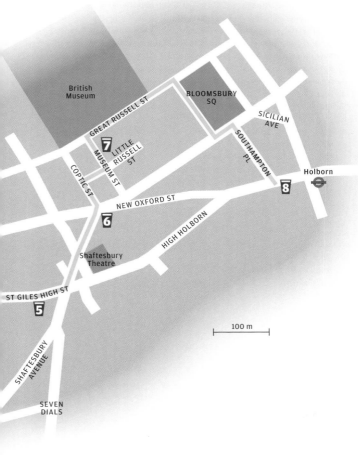

appears to have taken place in the 1930s. Don't miss the floor mosaic as you go in. If it's too crowded there is an upstairs room. This is apparently the pub where Madonna developed her taste for Timothy Taylor Landlord. Two other real ales, including Fuller's London Pride, are sold.

Now we retrace our steps to the little alleyway leading from Greek Street into Manette Street and reach the busy Charing Cross Road by Foyles bookshop. Directly opposite is Denmark Street, London's rather watered-down version of New York's Tin Pan Alley. For those interested in the history of pop and rock music, of course, this area is one of the capital's epicentres. Denmark Street quickly leads to St Giles High Street by the church of St Giles in the Fields. If you're seeking a brief rest, just behind the churchyard a gateway leads to the delightful little Phoenix Garden, an ecological refuge created from wasteland by dedicated volunteers. A little further along the High Street to the east lies the **Angel 5**. Behind the slightly

unprepossessing exterior lies one of the West End's best kept pub secrets, with a rare gem of an interior which still has three separate rooms and two separate street entrances. Tribute must yet again be paid to Yorkshire brewer Samuel Smith for an excellent and sensitive refurbishment in the 1990s when the pub was restored in a style close to its Edwardian character. Perhaps the highlight is the small rear saloon, accessed via the unusual enclosed side carriageway that also leads to a secluded little rear patio. As with all Sam Smith's pubs however, it's Hobson's choice as far as the beer is concerned: only Old Brewery Bitter in cask, but good value, unpretentious food is available.

Come out of the Angel, cross the road and bear left up Shaftesbury Avenue keeping the small green and the Shaftesbury Theatre on your right. [LINK]

The attractive **Bloomsbury Tavern 6**, another late Victorian pub and allegedly the last in London to have a 'wine only' licence, lies at the point where we join New Oxford

The handsome **Bloomsbury Tavern**

Street. Oddly enough, the handsome exterior with three substantial doorways suggests an interior far larger than the confined single space we find inside. It's now tied to Kent brewery Shepherd Neame, and keeps a wide range of their beers in good condition. Lunchtime food is available.

Cross over New Oxford Street into Coptic Street opposite and then take Little Russell Street on the first right. You may wish to make a brief diversion to view the eighteenth century St George's Church, Bloomsbury, which is one of Nicholas Hawksmoor's finest churches. It is just beyond the next crossroads on the right. However, remaining on the pub-hunting trail, turn left at the crossroads into Museum Street to bring us straight to our next pub, the **Museum Tavern 7**, which is right opposite the British Museum. Even though this was built in 1855, its refit of 1889 means that this is another pub whose style owes more to the late Victorian age. Surviving fixtures include the good bar back and counter (although all the mirrors but one

are replacements), while there is some nice stained and etched glass too. However, given the long narrow shape of the drinking area it's a pity that the dividing screens have as usual been removed. Up to five beers are usually on tap including Theakston's Old Peculier and a guest beer.

Upon leaving the Museum Tavern turn right to head eastwards along Great Russell Street for a short distance until we reach Bloomsbury Square on the right. This was the first of London's open spaces to be called a square and dates back as far as 1665. Walk round the square to Southampton Place, then cross Bloomsbury Way at the southern end, and down Southampton Place to join High Holborn. Almost opposite stands our last pub and a fitting finale to this architecturally rich trail. There is no doubt that the **Princess Louise 8** would be a highlight of any British pub walk. This late Victorian building was named after one of Queen Victoria's daughters and has some of the finest mirror and tile work to be seen in any pub. It is a

The **Princess Louise**, arguably London's finest tile and mirror work

Mirror by Morris of Kennington in the **Princess Louise**

testimony to the skills of the celebrated firms of R Morris and WB Simpson respectively. The rich mirrors represent a technique known as French embossing, which was applied with tremendous results here by Morris. The wonderful stillion with its pendant lights is probably the work of one WH Lascelles, and must surely be one of the finest survivors of its kind. What makes it even more special is that it can still be enjoyed without the intrusion of a glasses gantry on the counter to obstruct the view. The rich red lincrusta ceiling, attractive bar counter and appropriate seating are also all pleasing. The only things missing from the interior of this splendid pub are the screens, which undoubtedly would have divided the space into several compartments. Yet again Samuel Smith deserve praise for returning this now treasured building, which once was in a rather sorry condition, to its former glory. As is usual for Smith's London estate, Old Brewery Bitter is the only real ale available.

From here it is but a minute's walk along High Holborn to Holborn underground station, on the Piccadilly and Central lines. Or, if you prefer, there are buses to virtually all parts.

LINK Walk 9, **Covent Garden** (*page 43*). Upon leaving the Angel, turn right down the busy Shaftesbury Avenue and almost immediately left into Monmouth Street and follow straight down and across Seven Dials to join the walk at the Salisbury, St Martin's Lane.

PUB INFORMATION for walk 10 Centre Point Horseshoe – Fitzrovia, Soho & St Giles

1 Hope
15 Tottenham Street, W1
020 7637 0896
11–11 Mon–Sat; 12–6 Sun

2 Newman Arms
23 Rathbone Street, W1
020 7636 1127
11.30–11 Mon–Fri
Closed Sat and Sun

3 Tottenham
6 Oxford Street, W1
020 7636 7201
11–11 Mon–Sat; 12–10.30 Sun
CAMRA National Inventory

4 Dog and Duck
18 Bateman Street, W1
020 7494 0697
11–11 Mon–Sat; 12–10.30 Sun
CAMRA National Inventory

5 Angel
61 St Giles High Street, WC2
020 7240 2876
11–11 Mon–Sat; 12–10.30 Sun
CAMRA Regional Inventory

6 Bloomsbury Tavern
236 Shaftesbury Avenue, WC2
020 7379 9811
11–11 Mon–Sat; *Closed Sundays*

7 Museum Tavern
49 Great Russell Street, WC1
020 7242 8987
11–11 Mon–Sat
12–10.30 Sun
CAMRA Regional Inventory

8 Princess Louise
208 High Holborn, WC1
020 7405 8816
11–11 Mon–Sat
12–10.30 Sun
CAMRA National Inventory

WALK INFORMATION

Number of pubs: 6
Distance: 1 mile (0.6 km)
Key attractions: Soho, Oxford Street, Trocadero Centre, Chinatown, Regent's Park.
Beer range: ★/★★
Pub architecture: ★★/★★★
Links: to walk 10

This linear walk takes us from the southern end of Regent's Park towards Oxford Circus, finishing up in Soho. Expect to find good quality pub interiors, and plenty of shopping opportunities as we pass Oxford Street. Watch out for the Sunday pub closures on this trail, which is the longest of the three West End routes if you complete the whole length.

Start at Regent's Park underground station on the Bakerloo Line, or Great Portland Street station on the Metropolitan, Circle and Hammersmith and City lines. If you use this stop, exit the station and walk about 100 yards west down the Marylebone Road to Park Crescent.

Park Crescent was originally conceived by architect John Nash as a formal entrance to Regent's Park, but only the southern half was ever completed, and it is cut off from the park by the busy Marylebone Road. Walk down past its handsome terraces to Portland Place, which leads off from Park Crescent. This is a wide and majestic avenue, one of London's best, lined with houses in the Adam style. Clearly not in this style, but certainly noteworthy, is the headquarters of the Royal Institute of British Architects (RIBA) at no 66 on the corner of Weymouth Street. The interior of this Portland stone building is open to the public and there is a café and bookshop.

After all this culture, refreshment is close at hand. Cross Portland Place, turning right into Weymouth Street and first left into Weymouth Mews, where halfway down on the right is the well-hidden and attractive

Dover Castle 1. This is another of the carefully managed public houses in the estate of Samuel Smith. Dating back to 1750, it has apparently held a licence since 1777. The old wood-panelled interior has been opened out but retains its appealing atmosphere and there is some etched glass from its partitioned days. If you are a visitor to London, consider yourself lucky to have found the place. It's one of the most concealed of all London pubs, and many would-be patrons give up. As usual for Sam Smith, the only cask beer is Old Brewery Bitter.

Return to Portland Place by walking to the far end of Weymouth Mews, turning left, then right, and continuing to the end, past the distinctive church of All Souls, Langham Place. The road now becomes Regent Street and leads us directly towards Oxford Circus. Just before we get there, bear left onto Great Castle Street and along to your next pub, the **Cock Tavern 2**.

This is yet another Sam Smith's pub. Built at the start of the twentieth century, it certainly looks the part inside and out, especially now that Smith's have refitted it and returned it to something approaching its original splendour. A lot of what you see,

The restored interior of the **Cock Tavern**

Given its location so close to the bustle of Oxford Street, the survival of the stunning exterior and interior of this pub, built in 1868 and remodelled circa 1895, is quite remarkable. The striking exterior, with those distinctive curved windows, leads to a mirror-lined and terrazzo-floored corridor. In turn, compartments open up on the right with splendidly etched and cut screenwork. These small compartments are now very rare in pubs and are not to be missed here; these are the best of their kind left in London. The bar back is original, and note the tiny landlord's office halfway down.

To the rear of this large pub is a spacious room where the staircase is worth looking at for its ironwork. The beers here come from the larger brewers.

Continue down Argyll Street to Liberty's Tudor building at the bottom. This imposing edifice was constructed in 1922–3, coinciding with the Tudor revival's influence on pub

however, is not original. The screens inside are good examples of this; they look good but are replacements.

Come out of the pub and walk straight down to Oxford Street about 100 yards away. Wading through the shoppers, cross the road and turn right for a few yards before heading left into the pedestrianised Argyll Street just before the traffic lights. Note the distinctive Leslie Green tiled former entrance to the Underground station on the corner. Just a few yards further down is a pub which surely must be the architectural highlight of this walk, the **Argyll Arms 3**. The pub is named after one of the Duke of Marlborough's generals who was also a local landowner.

Front and interior drinking booths of the **Argyll Arms**

The imposing facade of the **Clachan**

design. It was made of timbers from *HMS Impregnable* and *HMS Hindustan* and still houses the famous arts and crafts store, which was founded in 1875. Turn right and then first left into Kingly Street. Here, well hidden in this quiet little side street parallel with nearby Regent Street, is the imposing facade of the **Clachan** . This is another late Victorian rebuild of 1898, which has managed to keep some of its original fittings including some rich wood-carving and structural iron-work. Look for the pretty tiling in the entrances. Note the cosy raised seating area at the back of the bar, which could conceivably have once been the landlord's parlour. The pub was formerly known as the *Bricklayers* and owned by Liberty, who had plans to turn it into a warehouse. You may be lucky enough to get Timothy Taylor Landlord here and the occa-sional guest offering, alongside beers from the likes of Greene King and Tetley's.

From the Clachan walk further down Kingly Street as far as the *Blue Posts* pub on the corner of Ganton Street, noting the rather handsome exterior with its leaded and stained glass. Turn left to reach and cross the pedestrianised Carnaby Street, now only a shadow of its former Swinging 60s self. Just a little further on the left is your next port of call, the **Shaston Arms** [5]. Stepping inside this inviting and intimate little pub, with its screened drinking booths and dark woodwork, one could be forgiven for thinking that this was one of London's hidden vintage

pubs. In fact, it has only been a pub for a decade, having been skilfully converted via a wine bar from shop premises. It is part of the Hall & Woodhouse estate so expect the likes of Badger Bitter and Tanglefoot on handpump.

Leaving the Shaston, turn left and then take the right turn into Marshall Street, turning first left into Broadwick Street. We're now walking towards the centre of Soho and as we pass the *John Snow* pub on the right there's an interesting little piece of history here. The pink granite kerbstone marks the site of the Broad Street pump where Snow, in an early example of applied geography, demonstrated with a map that an outbreak of cholera in Soho was the result of contamination of the water from this pump. Prior to this it was thought that cholera was an airborne disease. The pub itself has been very nicely restored even down to replaced screens by Samuel Smith and you may wish to have a peek inside, but be aware that there is no real ale to be had at present. Accordingly, continue along towards Broadwick Street to the Dutch-gabled pub at the end, which is another *Blue Posts*. It is claimed that the name referred to posts marking the boundaries of the Soho hunting ground, and even today there are four pubs in the district that carry this unusual name. Its exterior, with its Watneys lamps and frosted windows, looks very 60s and indeed you may well be drawn in for a quick visit. Rest assured that the demon ale produced by this once *bête noire* of CAMRA is no longer to be found inside. To your right is Berwick Street with its market, but to continue the trail, carry on

along Broadwick Street keeping the *Blue Posts* on your right to reach Wardour Street in a few yards. This is one of Soho's main thoroughfares, and is remembered by many for the golden years of the *Marquee Club* at No. 90, which hosted many of the great names of rock music from the 60s to the 80s. Closer to hand, indeed almost opposite, is the last pub in the walk, the **Ship** 6. This is one of Soho's best pubs and fittingly, for the area is very keen on its music. Those who belong to the aforementioned Marquee era can wallow in nostalgia here, for music from that era is frequently played, sometimes rather loudly. Dancing is not allowed though and there is an interesting tale about this, which you may be able to uncover by paying a visit! The place has an attractive interior with etched glass and mirrors, although most of what you see in is a post-war restoration following considerable wartime damage. This is Fuller's only Soho pub, so of course expect their range of beers.   [LINK]

From the Ship your best bet for public transport is to walk northwards towards Oxford Street. This will take about five minutes and buses will take you practically everywhere, including Central Line underground stations. Alternatively, follow Wardour Street southwards to Shaftesbury Avenue, which again takes about five minutes, and turn right for Piccadilly Circus underground.

Link Walk 10, Centre Point Horseshoe *(page 49)*. Come out of the Ship, cut through the narrow St Anne's Court nearby to Dean Street, turn right then first left into Bateman Street to arrive at the *Dog and Duck*.

PUB INFORMATION for walk 11 W1: Regent's Park to Soho

1 Dover Castle
43 Weymouth Mews, W1
020 7580 4412
11.30–11 Mon–Fri; 12–11 Sat
Closed Sundays
CAMRA Regional Inventory

2 Cock Tavern
27 Great Portland Street, W1
020 7631 5002
11.30–11 Mon–Sat; 12–10.30 Sun
CAMRA Regional Inventory

3 Argyll Arms
18 Argyll Street W1
020 7734 6117
11–11 Mon–Sat; 12–9.30 Sun
CAMRA National Inventory

4 Clachan
34 Kingly Street W1
020 7494 0834
11–11 Mon–Sat
Closed Sundays

5 Shaston Arms
4 Ganton Street, W1
020 7287 2631
11.30–11 Mon–Fri; 12–11 Sat
Closed Sundays

6 Ship
116 Wardour Street, W1
020 7437 8446
11–11 Mon–Sat
12–10.30pm Sun

WALK 12 **Belgravia**

WALK INFORMATION
Number of pubs: 7
Distance: 1.7 mile (2.5 km)
Key attractions: Hyde Park, Albert Hall, Victoria & Albert Museum, Knightsbridge shopping, Belgrave Square.
Beer range: ★★
Pub architecture: ★★
Links: to walks 5 and 25

Note: some pubs on this walk are not open at weekends, so plan accordingly.

A casual walk around the well heeled, but frankly rather soulless, streets of Belgravia may not at first reveal very much for the discerning drinker. In an eloquent testimony to the social status of the early Victorian pub, the area's builder Thomas Cubitt excluded them from everywhere in Belgravia except the mews, those little backstreet alleys hidden from immediate view. So it's no surprise that our first four pubs here are mews pubs off the beaten track.

Exit Victoria station, if possible, by the side exit to Buckingham Palace Road, or turn left and left again from the front exit. In one of the more difficult manoeuvres of this walk, cross the road and head down Lower Belgrave Street towards Belgrave Square. This area was laid out for the Earl of Grosvenor in the 1820s by Thomas Cubitt (1788–1855), one of the earliest and most important of London's speculative builders. He also laid out Kemp Town in Brighton and built Osborne House on the Isle of Wight for Queen Victoria. Pass Eaton Square and take the second right, Chester Street, before turning first left into Groom Place where you will find the **Horse & Groom** 1. It was opened in 1864 with the then clientele being the stable and mews workers of the gentry. It's a pleasant Shepherd Neame house with a small wood-panelled bar, while the food, especially the sandwiches, comes highly recommended. It is also reputed to have been a favourite haunt of Beatles' manager, Brian Epstein. Pity about the rather cheap laminate floor...

Return to Upper Belgrave Street and continue north-west, passing the handsome Belgrave Square on your left. At the end of the square continue ahead into Wilton Crescent before taking another mews turning, Wilton Row. This narrow defile brings you to one of the city's most sequestered pubs, the **Grenadier** 2, dating from around 1830.

The well-hidden **Grenadier**

It is quite likely that Wellington's guards from the nearby barracks used the place, but whether the Iron Duke himself did is open to question, since he was Prime Minister by 1828 and had switched military matters for politics by the time it was built. Certainly an old photograph in Mark Girouard's *Victorian Pubs* suggests far humbler origins than the smart building of today. The small front bar with its well worn floorboards and atmos-

pheric seating would have originally been divided up, as the side door suggests, and the once private rooms to the side and rear of the bar counter are now dining rooms, though without loss of character. Note the now very rare pewter bar top, and the old-fashioned handpulls, now redundant except for advertising the sort of wares that I hope you won't be drinking! Rest assured, however, that those alongside dispense the real McCoy including beers from Young's and Courage.

Leave the pub by the side alley, Barrack Yard, and turn left into another mews. If you follow this round, you should be able to exit onto Wilton Place. If, for any reason, the gates

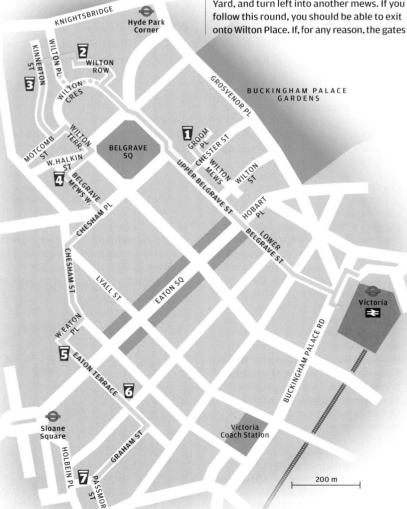

are closed simply return to Wilton Crescent and turn left and left again into Wilton Place. Cross over into Kinnerton Street, another mews, and as you turn left at the *Good Beer Guide*-listed *Wilton Arms*, which is worth a visit, you will see the **Nag's Head 3**. [LINK 1] This is a lovely old-fashioned urban pub, which was built in the 1830s and first licensed as a beer house shortly afterwards. It has lots of character, and is a genuine free house after a long innings as a Benskins house. These days it favours beers from Adnams. There are wood-panelled walls, floorboards, a fireplace with a range, and perhaps the lowest bar counter in London! As with so many pubs, new drinking areas have been brought into use by extending into once private quarters. In this case the pub has been extended up to a rear mezzanine and down into the basement, but without detriment to its distinctive character. The name reminds us that horses and carriages for the rich of Belgravia were stabled in the mews, and this would have been a pub for the stable-boys and footmen who lived hereabouts. There's an interesting collection of old penny-arcade machines, but I'm glad to say, no modern ones.

Continue down Kinnerton Street to Motcomb Street and turn left to the junction with Wilton Terrace. Before turning right down to the other corner of Belgrave Square, note the blue plaque on the first house left, indicating that Earl Mountbatten of Burma and his wife, Edwina, lived here. Turn right again at the square into West Halkin Street before taking the mews on the left, coming upon the **Star Tavern 4** almost immediately, a pleasant surprise indeed. This is one of my favourite London pubs, with a handsome frontage and a welcoming interior. Since 1951 it's been a Fuller's house, and been in every edition of CAMRA's *Good Beer Guide* so far. Again, an early nineteenth-century building that once would have been divided into several rooms, it is now popular with a range of customers and retains an upstairs bar as well as the main drinking areas below. Legend has it that this was the place where the Great Train Robbers planned their heist.

Continue down the mews to the German Embassy at the end and reach Chesham

The smart elevation of the **Star Tavern**

Place. If you've had your fill by now, you can return to Victoria in 10 minutes by turning left and right and continuing straight down Belgrave Place. However, to continue our tour, turn right and at the junction half left into Chesham Street, merging into Eaton Place and almost immediately taking the next right into West Eaton Place. Follow the road round, and in a couple of minutes you will reach the **Antelope 5**. On the outskirts of Belgravia and close to Sloane Square, the Antelope was, like the Nag's Head, also built for the household staff working in the grand houses, though there had apparently been a pub here before Cubitt developed the area.

The two separate entrances of the **Antelope**

Note the two separate entrances, a sign that it was originally divided into several bars. Some vestige of this layout can still be seen, although some of the areas like the room on the left have only been recently converted into use from private quarters. The rear area is attractive with a tiled fireplace and floorboards as well as high-backed benches. This handsome pub is one of the most recent acquisitions of Fuller's of Chiswick, who took over the licence in January 2005, so expect their excellent beers.

Continue down the street across the main road and you come very quickly to the **Duke of Wellington** 🖸, on a prominent corner site. This is yet another early Victorian pub, but reportedly it was originally opened as a library for employees of the Belgravian gentry. There are lots of old prints of the Iron Duke around the walls, as well as his mounting block, a chunk of granite carved by the

The **Duke of Wellington**

Duke's batman. The interior has been modernised and is now a single horseshoe bar and drinking area. The television can be rather obtrusive if switched on but the pub is a pleasant enough locals' pub, friendly and well run with reliable beers from the Shepherd Neame range.

To finish, continue down Eaton Terrace as far as Graham Terrace, the next road on the right, and turning here you will see the **Fox & Hounds** 🗷 just ahead. Until 1999, this former Charrington's pub was the last pub in London without a spirits licence. This quaint custom dated back to the Beer Act of 1830 and was at one time very common, put into place with the hope of luring the populace away from spirits. Young's have had the pub for the last decade or so, and have opened out the interior, creating something on the way to a café bar atmosphere, though some character still remains. Naturally, the real ales come from Young's.

From here, the easiest public transport option is to walk to the other end of Passmore Street and take bus numbers 11, 211 or 239 to Victoria. [LINK 2] Alternatively continue to the end of Graham Street and turn right into Holbein Place, it's then a short walk of about five minutes to Sloane Square underground station.

Link 1 Walk 25, **Hyde Park** (*page 115*). Turn right here, and left into Knightsbridge then follow this walk in reverse.

Link 2 Walk 5, **Westminster** (*page 25*). From Victoria, follow directions to this trail.

PUB INFORMATION for walk 12 **Belgravia**

🖥 Horse & Groom
7 Groom Place, SW1
020 7235 6980
11–11 Mon–Fri
Closed Saturday and Sunday

🖩 Grenadier
18 Wilton Row, SW1
020 7235 3074
12–11 Mon–Sat; 12–10.30 Sun
CAMRA Regional Inventory

🖪 Nag's Head
53 Kinnerton Street, SW1
020 7235 1135
11–11 Mon–Sat; 12–10.30 Sun

🖫 Star Tavern
6 Belgrave Mews West, SW1
020 7235 3019
11–11 Mon–Sat; 12–10.30 Sun

🖬 Antelope Tavern
22 Eaton Terrace, SW1
020 7824 8512
11.30–11 Mon–Fri; 12–11 Sat
Closed Sundays

🖭 Duke of Wellington
63 Eaton Terrace, SW1
020 7730 1782
11–11 Mon–Sat
12–10.30 Sun

🖮 Fox & Hounds
29 Passmore Street, SW1
020 7730 6367
11–11 Mon–Sat
12–10.30 Sun & bank holidays

WALK 13 St James's and Mayfair

WALK INFORMATION

Number of pubs: 5
Distance: 1.4 mile (2.3 km)
Key attractions:
Fortnum & Mason's,
Ritz Hotel,
St James's Park,
Buckingham Palace,
Museum of Mankind,
Royal Academy of Arts,
Berkeley Square.
Beer range: ★★
Pub architecture: ★★★
Links: to walk 11

This is one of London's richest areas and it has some pleasant backwaters. In some respects, its development at the start of the eighteenth century marked it out as one of the first of London's true suburbs. As we walk northwards through this very well-heeled area, the evidence of early town planning is still visible in the shape of elegant streets with formal squares, as well as mews for stable hands. The up-market retailers who followed the rich migrants westwards are still here, as we shall see. It's a relatively unfrequented area for the beer tourist, but there's much to see with our pubs ranging from the simple to the grand, and all of them having some architectural interest. Don't go on Sundays though – it's closed!

Start at St James's Park underground station – this will enable you to set the right tone by strolling across St James's Park to work up a nice thirst. Exit onto Broadway and take the street opposite, running away from the station, past the *Old Star* public house, and then use the pedestrian crossing to cross the inappropriately named Birdcage Walk.

St James's Park is the oldest of London's royal parks and started life as a hunting ground for Henry VIII, though the present park was landscaped by John Nash in the early nineteenth century. This route takes you on a traverse from south to north, crossing the bridge which affords attractive views of the London Eye to the right, and Buckingham Palace to the left through the trees. Keep on the same bearing and cross the Mall, which, unless its Sunday when it's closed to traffic, will be busy. Take the street opposite, Marlborough Road, past St James's

Palace, most of which is closed to the public as it is Prince Charles's private London pad. Across the street is Queen's Chapel, one of Inigo Jones's classical churches. All this culture and you'll be ready for a drink, so at the end of Marlborough Road as we emerge onto Pall Mall, look for an archway opposite in Quebec House. This is Crown Passage and home to an atmospheric little alleyway of shops and a pleasant pub, the **Red Lion** 🍺.

The **Red Lion**, Crown Passage

The frontage of the pub suggests a venerable age, perhaps the eighteenth century, and a rather presumptuous sign reads, 'London's last village pub.' The panelled interior, however, is probably a legacy of the 1930s, and although the pub is very small it would have been subdivided at one time as the two doorways suggest. The narrow stairs at the rear lead to a small dining room. All in all it is a civilised place away from the well-beaten tourist trail. Adnams' beers and Draught Bass are available.

Upon leaving the Red Lion and continuing up Crown Passage, you emerge onto King Street, home of well-famous auctioneers Christie's across the road. A few doors down to the right there is the second of three lions, this time the **Golden Lion** 2. Built by the prolific pub architects, Eedle & Meyers, in 1897–9, it sports a very attractive façade with bow windows, whilst the interior is small, solid and handsome, with a sturdy bar counter and gantry, wooden floors and

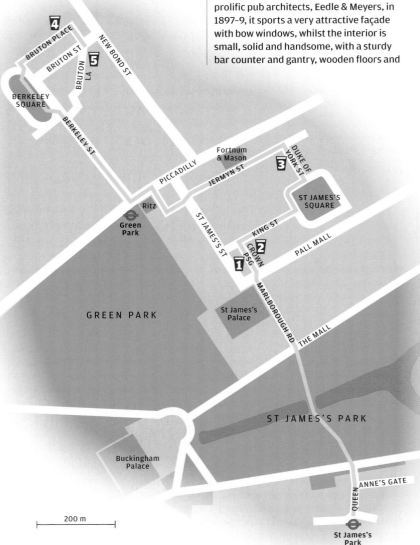

seating on stools. Young's, London Pride and Greene King IPA were available as well as Harvey's Sussex bitter on my last visit.

Stroll down King Street to St James's Square at the far end, which is one of London's many formal squares, and boasts a history as a very fashionable address. Number 10 was home to no less than three former prime ministers according to one of many blue plaques around the square. Take the road north from the square and we arrive a couple of minutes later at another **Red Lion** 3, one of the most splendid of the surviving Victorian pubs in London, and indeed in Britain. Although the building was constructed in 1821, both the pub's frontage and its interior are later in date. This is a veritable late Victorian cathedral of glass, mirrors and woodwork. The richness of the deeply-cut mirrors here is particularly impressive, as they glint and sparkle in the light. Yet, despite

the size, it is clear that the building had several internal divisions in the past, hence three doors at the front, each of which would have led into a separate compartment. A quasi-corridor leads to the rear room which is separated from the small front space by an island servery. Go as early as you can to enjoy the place as it can get quite crowded at lunchtimes as well as early evenings; but it quietens down later on. Several beers are usually available including London Pride and Timothy Taylor Landlord.

Come out and turn onto Jermyn Street by St James's church. This street has long been, and indeed still remains an epicentre of gentlemen's fashion, with shirts a speciality. As we walk along past elegant shop fronts, note the rear of Fortnum & Mason's to the right, and crossing St James's Street pass the heavily modernised *Blue Posts* pub. Turn right here and emerge on Piccadilly by the *Ritz Hotel*.

Rich internal fittings in the **Red Lion** in Duke of York Street

Walk along the frontage of the *Ritz* (you'll need about £20 and to book several weeks in advance to take afternoon tea here!), and cross the road into Berkeley Street opposite. If you've ever played Monopoly and wondered where Mayfair was, well, you're in it now. The famous Berkeley Square, immortalised in song, is five minutes ahead, though you will be very lucky to hear a nightingale above the noise of traffic these days. This is a pleasant place despite the traffic, with some lovely mature plane trees and lawns. A series of very handsome Georgian houses line the west side, in contrast to the brash temples of capitalism on the east. Leave the square at the north-east corner where you'll find Bruton Place, and down here, amidst the affluence of Mayfair, is a remarkable survivor down on the left, the **Guinea** 4. Remarkably,

The **Guinea** in Mayfair

given the surroundings, the old pub has been little adulterated and its interior still feels like the mews alehouse it once was, although food in the grill and dining room adjacent will set you back a pretty penny. The main bar area is still divided by a door and screen into two rooms; note the small etched glass panels. Furnishings are agreeably simple and the floor is uncarpeted; beers come from Young's. The dining area, beyond the smaller bar room, offers good food in a panelled room.

Leaving the Guinea, carry on around the corner to join Bruton Street, and the last pub on this walk sits on the corner. The **Coach & Horses** 5 seems to be relatively unknown, but behind the mock Tudor exterior, there is a nice quiet and compact pub, adorned with

lots of dark woodwork. There is a good beer list with a guest ale complementing a range of beers from familiar London brewers. Food is served until 9pm and there is an upstairs dining room open at lunchtimes.   **[LINK]**

From here, the nearest underground station is Green Park. Go down the diagonal Bruton Lane to the south east corner of Berkeley Square, left down Berkeley Street to Piccadilly and then right, but your best bet may be bus route 8 which passes the pub and seems to go just about everywhere.

Link Walk 11, W1: Regent's Park to Soho (*page 55*). From the Coach & Horses walk east, crossing Regent Street, into pedestrianised Foubert's Place. When you meet Carnaby Street, pick up the route.

PUB INFORMATION for walk 13 St James's and Mayfair

1 Red Lion
23 Crown Passage,
St James's, SW1
020 7930 4141
11–11 Mon–Sat
Closed Sundays
CAMRA Regional Inventory

2 Golden Lion
25 King Street, St James's, SW1
020 7925 0007
11–11 Mon–Sat
Closed Sundays

3 Red Lion
2 Duke of York Street,
St James's, SW1
020 7321 0782
11–11 Mon–Sat
Closed Sun & bank holidays
CAMRA National Inventory

4 Guinea
30 Bruton Place, W1
020 7409 1728
11–11 Mon–Fri; 12–6 Sat
Closed Sundays
CAMRA Regional Inventory

5 Coach & Horses (*detail below*)
5 Bruton Street, W1
020 7629 4123
11–11 Mon–Sat
Closed Sundays

WALK 14 **Marylebone**

WALK INFORMATION
Number of pubs: 6
Distance: 1½ miles (2.4 km)
Key attractions:
Planetarium,
Madame Tussaud's,
Sherlock Holmes
    Experience,
Sherlock Holmes Museum,
Oxford Street shopping.
Beer range: ★★
Pub architecture: ★/★★
Links: to walk 11

The district between Hyde Park and Regent's Park tends to be less frequented by visitors to London. Many of the Georgian streets and squares retain the elegance they had when the village of St Mary-by-the-Bourne was built over by its landowners a couple of centuries ago. Even today the High Street has a more local, village-like feel than is usual for London. The 'Bourne' in question was the Ty Bourne or Tyburn, of gallows fame, a stream running more or less on the modern line of Marylebone High Street and Marylebone Lane. Our walk is a north-west to south-east transect across Marylebone finishing at Bond Street. Some of the pubs do not open until noon, while others have restricted weekend hours, thus accounting for the eccentic route. If you are doing the route later in the day feel free to alter the order. The Barley Mow, certainly the most interesting interior on the trail, is closed on Sundays.

Start at Marylebone National Rail and underground station on the Bakerloo Line, or alternatively, take a bus on the Marylebone Road between Edgware Road and Baker Street stations and get off halfway between the two. Marylebone is one of the more attractive of the London termini, especially now that St Pancras has been ruined. Opened in 1899, it was the last to be built, and was part of a project that became the Great Central Railway, a competitor to the Midland, and part of a madcap venture to link up with a channel tunnel. A canopy still covers the station forecourt to link it with the old Great Central Hotel, now the *Landmark*, opposite.

Walk down Great Central Street to the busy Marylebone Road and use the crossing to reach Wyndham Street opposite, with the interesting St Mary's Church ahead. Walk around the church, and across the little square behind is your first pub, which is hard to miss given its gaudy red frontage. Do not let this put you off as the **Duke of Wellington** 🔲 is an attractive local which has earned its place in the *Good Beer Guide*. Inside, this surprisingly small pub has an intimate and refined atmosphere with a carpet and handsome seats. It's not the only pub on our route to have a collection of knick-knacks. Here, the window cabinets are

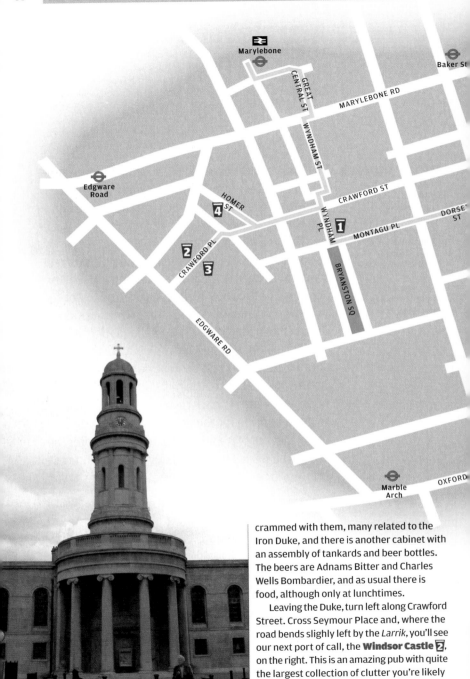

St Mary's Church in Bryanston Square

crammed with them, many related to the Iron Duke, and there is another cabinet with an assembly of tankards and beer bottles. The beers are Adnams Bitter and Charles Wells Bombardier, and as usual there is food, although only at lunchtimes.

Leaving the Duke, turn left along Crawford Street. Cross Seymour Place and, where the road bends slighly left by the *Larrik*, you'll see our next port of call, the **Windsor Castle 2**, on the right. This is an amazing pub with quite the largest collection of clutter you're likely to see in a London boozer. Even the ceiling is

PADDINGTON ST GARDENS

5

MANCHESTER ST

LANDFORD ST

BAKER ST

MARYLEBONE HIGH ST

NEW CAVENDISH ST

6

HINDE ST

MANCHESTER SQ

RTMAN SQ

WIGMORE ST

DUKE ST

Selfridges

Bond St

Madame Tussauds

London netarium

|———— 200 m ————|

food is well regarded. In good weather you can sit on the pavement benches outside. The pub, unusually, boasts its own chess club.

Retrace your steps back as far as Homer Street which is second left (beyond Homer Place), and peering up here you will spot a pub sign halfway up the street. This is the little **Beehive** **4** which boasts an attractive exterior. In an area of small pubs this is one of the smallest, but the welcome is warm, which is just as well as it feels very busy with just a few people inside. It retains some etched glass in the windows and a definite 'period' feel. Young's and Fuller's beers are on draught and there is food at lunchtime. This is an unpretentious pub which should not be missed.

The next leg is a longer walk but the end result is worth it. Go back to the Duke of Wellington, turn right into Wyndham Place, and at Bryanston Square turn left onto Montagu Place which, crossing busy Gloucester Place, becomes Dorset Street. Cross Baker Street, but beware, if you want to do the Sherlock Holmes thing it's no good looking for 221B; it doesn't exist. Frankly your best bet is probably the *Sherlock Holmes Experience* at no. 230 with a lot of artefacts from the 1980s TV series. There is also a museum at no. 239.

covered with glass cabinets full of plates! It's a friendly place with two real ales, Adnams and Bass, although the focus on Thai food can result in spicy aromas drifting into your beer. It's well worth a visit for the visual stimulation alone, however, and if you are lucky enough you may even see a fine moustache for this is the home of the *Handlebar Club*.

Almost across the road on the next corner is the **Wargrave Arms** **3**, a smart Young's house with a modernised and unexciting interior. The beer is fine, as you would expect from Young's, the service friendly and the

The attractive exterior of the **Beehive**

Just beyond the crossroads you will arrive at the **Barley Mow** 5 on a corner site. It was built in 1791 and claims to be the oldest pub in Marylebone. There are three external doors and a rear room with some very old panelling, but the *tour de force* here is the pair of small drinking boxes. It is claimed that these were used for pawnbroking transactions but they are very probably simply another example of the Victorian passion for privacy and are now unique in London.

Drinking boxes at the **Barley Mow**

Look out for the worn brass plates advertising liquor at very good value and the old bar back with the tap marked 'Old Tom'. Sadly, this was not the Stockport barley wine but a formerly popular variety of gin. Beers are from Adnams, Tetley and Greene King.

Turn left out of the pub and follow the road round to the right, where it becomes Manchester Street, then take the first left into Blandford Street. On reaching Marylebone High Street we veer on a right-left dog-leg as the High Street follows its crooked course, with our last official stop, the **Golden Eagle** 6, on the next corner. [LINK] This is a small, traditional local with basic, unfussy décor and one drinking area, and is deservedly popular with nearby workers. It serves lunchtime snacks but it's primarily what a pub should be for, drinking. Unusually here you can try beers from Cornish brewers St Austell.

The nicest route to public transport is to follow Marylebone High Street down to the next junction, turn right into Hinde Street and turn clockwise around Manchester Square into Duke Street. The square is named for the Duke of Manchester who, induced by the good duck-shooting in the area, built a house here in 1777. Today it's a handsome Georgian square with a fine collection of trees, shrubs and plants. If you are still game for another pub, try the little *Devonshire Arms* halfway down on the right, a 1930s pub with a decent range of beers. Just beyond is Oxford Street with numerous buses, and Bond Street underground station to your left.

Link Walk 11, W1: Regent's Park to Soho (*page 55*). From Marylebone High Street, follow a left-right course into New Cavendish Street, whence a five minute walk will bring you to the *Dover Castle* on Weymouth Mews.

PUB INFORMATION for walk 14 **Marylebone**

1 Duke of Wellington
94a Crawford Street, W1
020 7724 9435
11–11 Mon–Sat; 12–10.30 Sun

2 Windsor Castle
27–29 Crawford Place, W1
020 7723 4371
11–11 Mon–Sat; 12–10.30 Sun

3 Wargrave Arms
40–42 Brendon Street, W1
020 7723 0559
12–11 Mon–Sat; 12–10.30 Sun

4 Beehive
7 Homer Street, W1
020 7262 6581
12–11 Mon–Sat; 12–10.30 Sun

5 Barley Mow
8 Dorset Street, W1
020 7935 7318
11–11 Mon–Sat; Closed Sunday
CAMRA National Inventory

6 Golden Eagle
59 Marylebone Lane, W1
020 7935 3228
11–11 Mon–Sat; 12–7 Sun

WALK 15 **E1: Spitalfields to Whitechapel**

WALK INFORMATION
Number of pubs: 6
Distance: 1¼ miles (2 km)
Key attractions: Brick Lane, Christ Church, Spitalfields Market, Whitechapel Gallery, Whitechapel Market, Spitalfields City Farm, Fournier Street.
Beer range: ★★/★★★
Pub architecture: ★★
Links: to walk 2

This interesting trail doubles as a geography field trip on the process of gentrification, which is now in full swing in the area east of the A10 artery in the East End. It's an enjoyable stroll through markets, a richly mixed ethnic area and importantly one with some interesting pubs which reflect the diverse geography. Also, the pubs are open all week, so you can safely go at the weekend. The curries are good too, although maybe better *after* the beer!

Start at Liverpool Street Station, where there are several underground lines and National Rail. It has been said that any pub within 500 yards of a major rail terminal is never worth a visit. Certainly the *Hamilton Hall*, a large Wetherspoon's in the station, suffers from the surges of transient punters who swarm in, so best give it a miss and exit onto Bishopsgate. Across the road and slightly to the left you will spot a famous old pub, **Dirty Dick's** 🍺. The pub is named after Nathaniel Bentley, whose bride-to-be died on the eve of their wedding. Naturally, this caused the man great distress and he locked up the room he had prepared for their feast. It's also said that Bentley never changed his clothes again and left his cats where they died. When the place was rebuilt in about 1870 all the clutter was relocated in the 'new' pub and continued gathering dust until about 20 years ago, when the place fell foul of environmental health regulations and most of the offending artefacts were cleared away. Today's cleaned-up pub is pleasant and characterful enough with bare floorboards and an abundance of timber beams. The

The entrance to **Dirty Dick's**

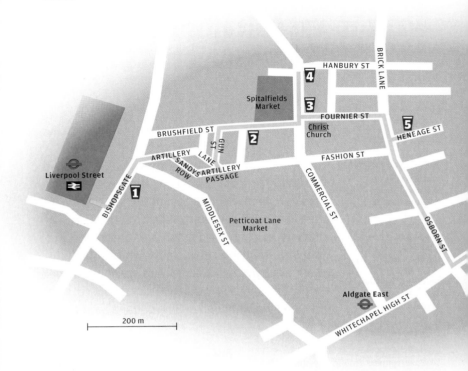

upstairs bar forms a gallery and the vaulted cellar a restaurant. Young's beers are on tap.

Head to the right of Dirty Dick's and take the second right into Artillery Lane. The name recalls the old artillery training ground that occupied an area just beyond here. This was just outside the City of London whose boundary with the parish of Spitalfields is marked by the first pair of iron bollards. Turn right into Sandy's Row, past the old Dutch synagogue, one relic of the large Jewish community that settled here in the nineteenth century. First left is the characterful Artillery Passage, following the old southern boundary of the Artillery Ground. Indeed at the far end, above no. 9, you can see one of the old boundary markers, dating from 1682 when the ground was sold and redeveloped. Swing left here, and first right is Gun Street, which supposedly follows the alignment of the old gunnery range. Follow Gun Street to its junction with Brushfield Street where you turn right. The range once

carried on northwards, beyond what is now Brushfield Street, but now this area is occupied partly by the old Spitalfields market, standing cheek by jowl with a new piazza and offices. Spitalfields is one of London's oldest markets dating back to the thirteenth century, and due to its original location becoming cramped it moved to Leyton in May 1991. That's one story anyway. The other is that this large site was being eyed up by developers, lying as it does between the expanding City on one side and run-down ripe-for-regeneration Tower Hamlets on the other. A sort of stand-off has seen half of the market lost and the remainder surviving as a general market selling antiques, crafts and food inside part of the splendid old market building. What's undeniable is the rapid pace of change in the area, so by the time you read this, things may have moved on, and that goes for the pubs too.

The **Gun** 2, halfway down the road, is a traditional, unpretentious corner boozer that

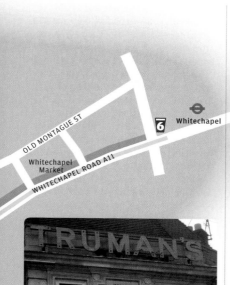

the *Jack the Ripper*. In sharp contrast to the decidedly shabby exterior with its old Truman livery peeling away, the interior has been given a serious makeover with mandatory leathery sofas, low tables, candles and musak. Though given that the clientele is changing to match, it can't be long before the outside gets an equally smart refurbishment. At some times of the day tour parties vie with bright young things, although I assume the sign on the door saying *no tour groups over 10* refers to size and not age! At quieter times it has a pleasant ambience and although they usually only have one draught beer it's often an interesting one and St Peter's organic beers are available in bottle. However, the real gem here is the blue and white tiling by the celebrated Victorian firm of Simpsons over the interior walls and a lovely old tiled picture, *Spitalfields in the Olden Time*, adjacent.

Our next pub is no further than the next corner. Turn right out of the Ten Bells and walk up to the **Golden Heart 4** on the corner of Hanbury Street. This is a prominent corner pub with another Truman fascia (*left*) and the old brewery site is opposite. It's also another pub in the throes of change, one feels, with a mixed clientele of locals, younger arty types and city suits. The chirpy long-serving landlady is a characterful East End type though, and the pub is welcoming to all. It has been described as 'one of the last bastions of a community and culture in retreat'. There are still separate rooms, and other features to look out for are the simple 1930s furnishings

has so far resisted the temptation to go too far into the sofa-and-Pimms part of the market. It's no architectural jewel but a small separate room survives to one side with old-fashioned wainscotting, a spittoon and footrail. It's a pity that a pool table almost fills this little room. The main bar is comfortable, with Adnams and Young's beer available. Outside, like several pubs in this area, the old Truman's fascia, complete with lamps, has survived. The site of the old brewery, once the world's largest but closed in 1989, is very close by.

Walk down the street with the impressive baroque elevation of Hawksmoor's Christ Church (1715–29) in front of you. The story goes that when it acquired more bells in its peal than Wren's St Bride's in Fleet Street, the public house opposite was renamed to celebrate. Today the **Ten Bells 3**, is a metaphor for the changing social character of Spitalfields. This is perhaps the most famous pub in the lucrative Jack the Ripper story, and from 1976 to 1988 it was even known as

The bar of the **Golden Heart**

and panelling, and some interesting exterior glass. There is also an unusual waist-height set of doors in the wall which allow access to the cellar trap just inside. Beers are from Adnams, alongside guests from the likes of Crouch Vale. Wooden plaques on the walls advertise bygone beers from the Truman range like Oatmeal Stout. To add to it all, there is an old-fashioned juke box, another increasingly rare sight in a pub these days.

Walk back down to the Ten Bells and take Fournier Street on the left, to admire the early Georgian terraced housing in one of London's most complete eighteenth century streets. At the far end of this short street you emerge into the heart of the Bangladeshi community of Brick Lane. If you are not familiar with this area you'll find it a thriving and colourful neigbourhood with a long history, predating the arrival of the Bangladeshi community. Originally the site of the kilns for the bricks that rebuilt London after the Great Fire, the area was a Jewish ghetto at the start of the twentieth century. Gentrification has arrived here too, as one can verify simply by looking at the furnishings and the prices in the numerous restaurants. Turn right and first left is Heneage Street, with our next pub tucked in just a few yards down. the **Pride of Spitalfields** 5 was formerly the Romford Arms, not a sustainable name maybe, with its connections with advertising-icon George, the infamous Hofmeister-drinking bear of the 80s. It's something of an institution in these parts, and a firm favourite with traditional beer fans. It too has been smartened up but not too much. Despite the carpets and red velour seats, and 'Mary's pantry' alongside the bar, it's a friendly and well

regarded local with a very good cellar, from which Fuller's London Pride and ESB, Crouch Vale Brewer's Gold and a guest beer are dispensed. The walls are lined with interesting pictures of bygone East End life.

Continue down Brick Lane to the southern end, which these days is the heart of 'Bangla Town', and then turn left onto the Whitechapel Road. It's a good 10-minute stroll to our last pub, but along an increasingly interesting street as we approach Whitechapel Market. Whitechapel was one of the largest Victorian street markets and was mainly run by Jewish and Irish traders. However, it is now a South Asian market open Monday to Saturday with nearly 100 stalls selling everything from fresh fruit to fish, clothing, bedding, carpets, jewellery and electrical goods. Even more heartening, there is not a patisserie or three-wheeled buggy in sight. Almost opposite the Royal London Hospital, across a set of traffic lights, the **Black Bull** 6 awaits us. The local CAMRA pub of the year in 2005, it has a modernised, opened-out interior with little architectural interest, but nonetheless it's a showcase for well kept ales from the Nethergate Brewery in Suffolk and a very rare London outlet for their beers. The large TV is not a welcome feature but the pub is worth it for the ethnic tour and the beer.

Whitechapel Station on the Underground is a few yards further along the road when you have had your fill. Alternatively, the useful no. 25 bus across the road heads back towards Oxford Street via Holborn. [LINK]

Link Walk 2, **Heart of the City** (*page 13*). Use the no. 25 bus and jump off in Cornhill where you can roll into the start of the trail.

PUB INFORMATION for walk 15 **E1: Spitalfields to Whitechapel**

1 Dirty Dick's
202 Bishopsgate, EC2
020 7283 5888
11–11 Mon–Fri
Closed Saturday; 12–3 Sun

2 Gun
54 Brushfield Street, E1
020 7247 7988
11–11 Mon–Sat; 12–9 Sun

3 Ten Bells
Commercial Street, E1
020 7366 1721
11–11 Mon–Sat; 12–10.30 Sun
CAMRA Regional Inventory

4 Golden Heart
110 Commercial Street, E1
020 7247 2158
11–11 Mon–Sat; 12–10.30 Sun
CAMRA Regional Inventory

5 Pride of Spitalfields
3 Heneage Street, E1
0207 247 7988
11–11 Mon–Sat; 12–10.30 Sun

6 Black Bull
199 Whitechapel Road, E1
020 7247 6707
11–11 Mon–Sat; 12–10.30 Sun

Greenwich: a two hemispheres trail

WALK INFORMATION
Number of pubs: 6
Distance: 1½ miles (2.5 km)
Key attractions: *Cutty Sark*, *Gipsy Moth IV*, Greenwich Royal Observatory, Greenwich Market, National Maritime Museum, Meridian Line.
Beer range: ★★★
Pub architecture: ★★
Links: to walk 24

Greenwich is one of London's most popular tourist attractions and it's easy to see why. The area's unique maritime connections make it a worthy World Heritage Site, but it also has tremendous parkland, excellent views, fine vernacular architecture, a market and interesting shops. It is also richly endowed with pubs.
On top of all this, you can drink in both the eastern and the western hemisphere on one short walk.

Before setting out, it might be worth clicking on www.greenwichwhs.org.uk to have a look at the excellent map of historic Greenwich produced by the local authority. The recommended way to do Greenwich properly is to make a day of it and you can arrive in style by river from central London. For the river services, www.tfl.gov.uk/river is the website to check. Otherwise travel by Docklands Light Rail to Cutty Sark, or National Rail to Greenwich and make your way down to the quayside by the *Cutty Sark* itself. This book cannot attempt to do justice to the sights of Greenwich and a proper guide is recommended if you also plan to do a spot of sightseeing.

The *Cutty Sark* is a name with which most visitors to Greenwich will be familiar. She was the fastest sailing ship of her day and after being launched at Dumbarton in 1869 she initially sailed the tea route to China, once doing the trip from Shanghai in just 107 days. Later on, she brought back wool from Australia, but has been in dry dock in Greenwich since 1954. There are good views towards central London from the piazza by the riverside here and familiar buildings will be recognisable.

🏃 **It's time for a drink,** so head up past the *Cutty Sark*, past the *Gypsy Moth* pub and turn left at the Shepherd Neame-owned *Spanish Galleon* on the first corner into College Approach. You will see the handsome rendered elevation of the **Admiral Hardy** 1 about 100 yards down on the opposite side.

The **Admiral Hardy**

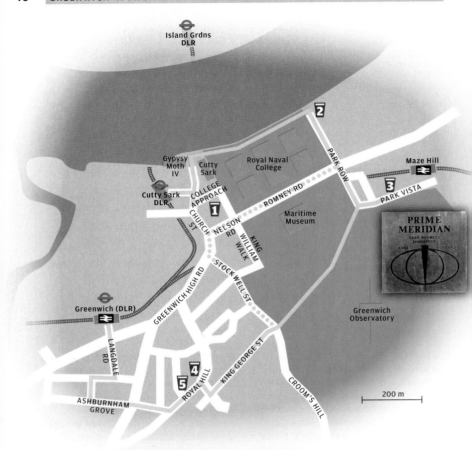

Named after the captain of *HMS Victory*, the key ship in the Battle of Trafalgar, the main interest in this heavily made-over free house is the unusual beer range, which includes beers from the Nelson Brewery in Kent, as well as other guests, often from Staffordshire brewers Eccleshall. The current interior style is casual and comfortable, as epitomised by yet more leathery sofas that seem to be springing up all over London. This is especially so in the nicely atmospheric rear room, which in good weather opens directly onto the courtyard occupied by Greenwich Market. Lunchtime food is available, and this is the best time to enjoy the place as it gets very full in the evenings. However, if you are in the market for food, my recommendation is to head to one of Greenwich's most venerable

institutions. Retrace your steps to the *Spanish Galleon* and across the street you will see Goddard's pie shop, a long-established stalwart of the area that has been going since 1890, serving honest-to-goodness pies, mash, peas and liquor at very reasonable prices in clean but thoroughly unpretentious premises. Goddard's is excellent value in a very pricey town, and long may they continue.

Return to the *Cutty Sark*, and beyond it take the Thames Path right (eastwards) as it skirts the impressive collection of buildings making up the Old Royal Naval College. This leads along the riverside to Greenwich's most famous inn, the massive **Trafalgar Tavern** 🔲, which has a prime waterfront site all to itself. The place dates back to 1837, the year Queen Victoria succeeded to the throne. Along with other local taverns it became famous for its whitebait suppers, which were a favoured delicacy with the politicians of the day and a tradition that still continues in the Trafalgar. However, the pub has also seen hard times and in 1915 it became a seamen's hostel, then later a working men's club. It was refurbished and reopened in 1965, winning a Civic Trust award. Today it is full of tourists, many of whom would not normally patronise a pub, but notwithstanding that it's worth a visit if only for the great riverside location. The Trafalgar occupies the site of an older pub, *The George*, and the ghost that haunts the bar is said to be a contemporary of this earlier alehouse. He is apparently seen in Georgian attire before getting up and walking through the wall where the fireplace was. Beers are well kept, as testified by the *Good Beer Guide* entry in 2006, and include the likes of Fuller's London Pride.

Head 'inland' up Park Row and cross the main road towards the park entrance ahead, following the road left at 90° by the park gates into Park Vista, to catch sight of our next quarry, the **Plume of Feathers 3**. This attractive street was at one time the main east-west route through Greenwich, dividing the park from the Tudor palace that stood by the river. Just before you reach the pub, look out for the meridian line, set as series of studs in the road leading to a metal groove in the footpath and a wall plaque. So once you are safely inside the Plume, the easternmost entry in this guide, you will have drunk in both hemispheres in one day! This agreeable pub dates from 1691 and not surprisingly, given its location, contains many naval artefacts. Beers come from the likes of Adnams and Fuller's, while food is available in the rear dining area.

Retrace your steps past the meridian and through the park gates, which are open during daylight hours. Head right at an angle of about 45° up across the park towards the King George Gate. A highly worthwhile detour, of course, is straight up the hill to the Greenwich Royal Observatory, where there are stunning views across London. Entry is now free as well, although you may have to compete with hundreds of other tourists and schoolchildren. Keeping on the trail though, walk a few yards downhill from King George Gate to turn into the road of the same name.

To get here when the park gates are closed, follow the road back down to the A206 main road you crossed earlier. Turning left, skirt the highly impressive National Maritime Museum, which is well worth a visit, and turn right along to the busy junction at the end of this road, keeping Greenwich market on your right. Turn left again here, and immediately fork left into Stockwell Street which becomes Crooms Hill. King George Street is the third turning on the right.

Walk along this handsome residential road before taking Royal Place, the first right, which takes us quickly down to a very welcome sight, two attractive pubs sitting literally cheek-by-jowl. The more imposing **Richard I 4** is the only Young's house on this trail and is an attractive and welcoming two-bar pub with unusual bay windows. Inside, there is lots of dark woodwork, so if you want more light try the large garden which naturally is very popular in summer. It's a regular entry in the *Good Beer Guide* so expect the Young's beers to be on form. The pub nickname, Tolly's, derives from its past association with the now defunct Ipswich-based brewery Tolly Cobbold.

Spoilt for choice in Greenwich

It is but a few yards to the next pub, the very different **Greenwich Union** 5. Owned and run by the local Meantime Brewery, the Union has been given a very modern makeover, which seems to work well for most visitors. The brewery produces some very interesting beers, many of them versions of classic world styles. They are dispensed under pressure, though, but the house Blonde is a cask-conditioned exception.

On my last visit for this guide, however, they also had a cask-conditioned 7.2% Porter on sale, which was full of taste and plenty of punch. Attentive staff and an interesting menu complement the appealing wet menu.

For our last port of call, walk up Royal Hill beyond the Union, taking the right fork but still remaining on Royal Hill, where Blisset Street continues ahead. Here, cross the main road at the foot of the hill into Ashburnham Grove opposite. The agreeable terraces of Victorian houses lining this street have made it one of Greenwich's most sought-after residential areas and, to complete the attractive scene, it has its own pub halfway along. The **Ashburnham Arms** 6 is a *Good Beer Guide* regular, and continues to flourish under its relatively new management. Given its affluent regulars, this Shepherd Neame house is refreshingly unpretentious and retains much of its three-room layout. Floorboards prevail and sofas coexist with bar stools. A spacious garden to the rear offers a summer retreat and a new development is a downstairs room devoted to games. Bar food is available, along with newspapers. All in all this is a very civilised place to end a varied tour around this historic location.

Fortunately it's only a short stroll down to the station. Take the street at the side of the pub and turn right into Ashburnham Place, then left into Langdale Road. Greenwich station is straight ahead of you across the main road (Docklands Light Rail and National Rail). [LINK]

Link Walk 24, **Riverside** (*page 109*). If time and money permit, take the river boat back to Tower Bridge and do this trail in reverse.

PUB INFORMATION for walk 16 **Greenwich: a two hemispheres trail**

1 Admiral Hardy
7 College Approach, SE10
020 8858 6452
12–11 Mon–Sat; 12–10.30 Sun

2 Trafalgar Tavern
Park Row, SE10
020 8858 2437
11–11 Mon–Sat; 12–10.30 Sun

3 Plume of Feathers
19 Park Vista, SE10
020 8858 0533
11–11 Mon–Sat; 12–10.30 Sun

4 Richard I
52–54 Royal Hill, SE10
020 8692 2996
11–11 Mon–Sat; 12–10.30 Sun

5 Greenwich Union
56 Royal Hill, SE10
020 8692 6258
11–11 Mon–Sat; 12–10.30 Sun

6 Ashburnham Arms
25 Ashburnham Grove, SE10
020 8692 2007
12–11 Mon–Sat; 12–10.30 Sun

WALK INFORMATION
Number of pubs: 6
Distance: 1 mile (1.6 km)
Key attractions: London Wildfowl and Wetland Centre, Fuller's Brewery, Hammersmith shops, Furnival Gardens and riverside.
Beer range: ★★
Pub architecture: ★★
Links: to walk 26

If the only experience you've ever had of Hammersmith is the hideous flyover and the traffic snarl-ups on the roundabout, you could be forgiven for thinking that this is the last place you'd ever want to come for a pub trail. But believe me, there are still some pleasant corners in old Hammersmith and this trail will visit some of them, whilst avoiding the central inferno! This is the closest route, too, to the excellent London Wetland centre, with 105 acres of wetland habitats. Take a 283 bus from stand C in central Hammersmith at the start or end of the trail. See www.wwt.org.uk.

Take the underground as far as Ravenscourt Park station on the District Line and on exit walk down to King Street. From here, turn left and just a little way along, where King Street becomes one-way, is your first port of call, the **Salutation** 🗍, with its distinctive lilac-tiled frontage advertising Fuller's Brewery. The spacious, opened-out interior, where little survives of the original pub, is not unpleasant, and there is a mixed bag of seating arrangements, including the almost mandatory leather sofas. It's a pity about the irritating piped music, but if the weather permits you can escape outside where there's a pleasant patio garden. This pub is one of the earliest documented in the Fuller's estate, acquired by Thompson, Wood & Fuller as they then were, in April 1824. It's still a Fuller's pub today so expect their beers, and the food comes recommended.

Just a little further east along King Street is an unusual Wetherspoon's pub, which was the site of a former pub before being demolished and replaced by a car showroom. The new **Plough & Harrow** 🔁 is a fiercely modern

Stainless-steel bar at the **Plough & Harrow**

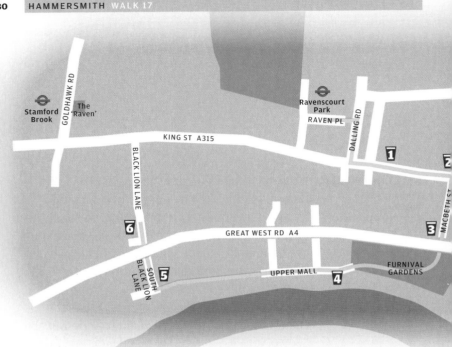

affair, but as is common with many other Wetherspoon's conversions, the chain has spent heavily in doing a good job. The stainless steel bar, for instance, with its glass decoration, may well be the sort of feature that tomorrow's pub architecture devotees will rave about. Note also the stainless steel fireplace. There is usually a wide range of beers and it's worth knowing that the pub opens from 10 am for breakfast as well as for beers.

Cross King Street and enter Macbeth Street, which is almost opposite. In a minute or two you'll see your next destination, the **Hope & Anchor** 3. This former Truman's pub is a very rare and almost intact survivor of the 1930s and has recently been statutorily listed Grade II as well as being added to CAMRA's *National Inventory of Historic Pubs and Interiors*. It's a pleasantly unpretentious pub, which retains a two-room layout, with

Fireplace at the **Plough & Harrow**

The **Hope & Anchor**

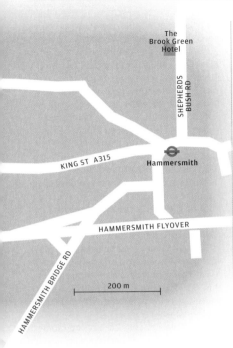

a public bar at the front and a rear saloon. The panelling, counter and bar back are original, as are the Truman's mirror and clocks. Note also the lettering advertising the brewery's long-gone ales (see also here the *Golden Heart*, Spitalfields, walk 15, page 73) and don't miss the chequered spittoon in the saloon, or the reeded glass windows. Fuller's London Pride is the real ale normally available although sometimes others appear.

One further feature of interest is the pleasant back yard with its neoclassical colonnade.

At the far end of Macbeth Street, take the subway under the noisy Great West Road, bearing right at the exit to enter Furnival Gardens. Named after Dr Frederick Furnival, an eminent Victorian philanthropist who lived in the area, and a great spot to watch the Cambridge-Oxford Boat Race, this small open space fronting the river provides a glimpse of the pleasant spot that Hammersmith once was. Walking through the gardens to the west, you will probably spot the sign of your next pub peering out from a cluster of old buildings on the Riverside. Indeed this pub, the **Dove** 🄴, is without doubt the best known in the area. This place, formerly the *Doves*, boasts a long list of celebrity customers, although separating fact from fiction is not always easy. Alexander Pope, Joseph Addison and Richard Steele, as well as artists like Joseph Turner and William Morris, all used the place according to a pub history produced by its owners Fuller's. Graham Greene, Ernest Hemingway and AP Herbert are all fairly well documented patrons too. Its age is less certain, but it is claimed that a pub has stood here for over 500 years. The current building is likely to be early to mid eighteenth century and, although much extended, it's still an intimate and delightful place to drink, especially during quieter parts of the day. The tiny snug is perhaps the smallest drinking room left in Britain, while the larger room with its old benches has some

The **Dove** (*above and right*)

of the oldest panelling of any London pub. Note the more modern fireplace from 1948, with its interesting stone carving. The rear room is set aside for eating and beyond here lies a small but agreeably sited terrace overlooking the river. Having been in the hands of Fuller's since 1848 it sells their range of beers.

Continue to follow the Thames Path for a quarter of a mile westwards towards Chiswick. Adjacent to a large outside drinking area and an ancient chestnut tree, you will spot a nicely sited little pub, the **Black Lion 5**. It used to be famous for its skittle alley, which is now used merely as a seating area; you can spot it by the long, narrow shape and boarded, shaped white ceiling. The pub itself has been smartened up in a refurbishment, although it still retains a good deal of its former character. It is complemented externally by some attractive brick terraced houses nearby. The pub at one time was the regular drinking hole of author AP Herbert but, unlike him, you don't have to drink Watneys, the demon keg bitter that helped to inspire the launch of CAMRA. The place now offers Courage Best Bitter, Greene King IPA and Wells Bombardier, as well as food.   [LINK]

Leaving the pub, walk up Black Lion Lane and for a second time negotiate the Great West Road by subway to emerge within sight of your next port of call, the **Cross Keys 6**. Situated in a residential street, this pleasant local was acquired by Fuller's in 1898 and has been in their estate ever since. It has a panelled interior that may date from the interwar period although, like the etched windows, it could be more modern.

Note the tiling in the former lobby as you enter the pub. Fuller's beers again.

Leaving the Cross Keys and continuing up Black Lion Lane brings you back onto King Street. Buses across the road will deliver you back to Hammersmith, whilst Stamford Brook underground is a couple of minutes' walk if you turn left and then right at the lights. Those with room for another drink could try the *Raven* just by the station. This is an old but heavily modernised pub which has a varying range of guest beers.

One further option, for those with a liking for interesting interiors, is the *Brook Green Hotel* on the Shepherd's Bush Road. Omitted from the trail proper because to get to it you will have to negotiate the centre of Hammersmith, which is not something I would lightly wish upon any reader, it's nonetheless worth a visit. Owned by Young's and featuring in the 2006 *Good Beer Guide*, it boasts some interesting features in its opened-out interior, not least the bar back with its green man carvings, the elaborate cornices and some good stained glass. To get here, take the bus back into Hammersmith and walk up the Shepherd's Bush Road northwards past the Hammersmith Palais for about five minutes. The pub is opposite the small green and opens early for breakfast (now there's a thought!)

Link Walk 26, Chiswick and Turnham Green (*page 119*). On leaving the Black Lion, it's a short walk of less than half a mile to join the end of the trail at the *Duke of Devonshire*. Simply follow the Thames Path further along the river to the end of Chiswick Mall, and turn up Church Road. You can then do the Chiswick route in reverse.

PUB INFORMATION for walk 17 **Hammersmith**

1 Salutation	**3 Hope & Anchor**	**5 Black Lion**
154 King Street, W6	20 Macbeth Street, W6	2 South Black Lion Lane, W6
020 8748 3668	020 8748 1873	020 8748 2639
11–11 Mon–Sat	12–11 Mon–Sat; 12–10.30 Sun	12–11 Mon–Sat
12–10.30 Sun	*CAMRA National Inventory*	12–10.30 Sun
2 Plough & Harrow	**4 Dove**	**6 Cross Keys**
120–124 King Street, W6	19 Upper Mall, W6	57 Black Lion Lane, W6
020 8735 6020	020 8748 5405	020 8748 3541
10am–11pm Mon–Sat	11–11 Mon–Sat; 12–10.30 Sun	12–11 Mon–Sat
10–10.30 Sun	*CAMRA Regional Inventory*	12–10.30 Sun

WALK 18 **Around Smithfield**

WALK INFORMATION
Number of pubs: 6
Distance: 1¼ mile (2 km)
Key attractions:
Smithfield Market,
St Bartholomew's Church,
Charterhouse.
Beer range: ★★
Pub architecture: ★★★
Links: to walk 23

This is a walk full of interest in a lesser-known part of London. It circumnavigates the great structure of Smithfield Market, once the largest meat market in the land, and passes the great ecclesiastical treasure of St Bartholomew's church. There are other notable landmarks, not to mention a variety of excellent pubs. Some of these are closed at weekends so it's a walk to enjoy during the week. Note also the earlier evening closure of several of the pubs. Some of them will have been open from the early hours for breakfast, so you can hardly blame them!

Start at Farringdon station on Thameslink National Rail and the Underground. Upon exit from the station, turn right and walk down to the Farringdon Road by the *John Oldcastle* pub. Turn left, then first right onto Charterhouse Street, before turning right again into the curious Ely Place with its gated and guarded entrance. To get to this point from Chancery Lane underground station on the Central Line, head eastwards down High Holborn to Holborn Circus, and Ely Place is the first turning left after crossing into Charterhouse Street.

The first pub on this walk is one of the hardest to find in London, since it lies down a tiny alley between numbers 9 and 10 Ely Place. In fact, given its history the **Old Mitre** 🚇 might well feel like a separate kingdom. The original tavern is said to have been built in 1546 for the servants of the nearby palace of the Bishops of Ely, and technically the pub was for years part of the county over which

The secluded **Old Mitre**

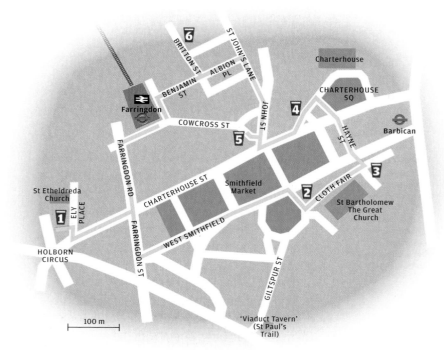

they presided. Until the late 1970s Cambridgeshire was the licensing authority for the pub! The nearby palace, the oldest Roman Catholic church in the city, was demolished in 1772 along with the pub, although the latter was rebuilt soon afterwards. The preserved trunk of a cherry tree, which allegedly marked the boundary of the Bishop of Ely's property, can still be detected in the corner of the small front bar of this very atmospheric hostelry. The interior you see today, replete with wood panelling throughout, dates back to an inter-war refitting, and a rare outside Gents' toilet completes the scene. The larger back room has a cosy snug. The beer range here usually comprises Tetley Bitter and offerings from Adnams.

Returning to Charterhouse Street, walk back up to the traffic lights and turn right, crossing the road before taking the first left into West Smithfield. You are now walking alongside the old Smithfield Market. This is a famous spot in the history of London, with a market having existed here since the twelfth century. Older still was the famous

Bartholomew Fair, which was a cloth fair originally founded to fund the famous Bart's hospital nearby. The site was also used for jousting and was notorious as a place of execution during the Reformation. In the nineteenth century, Smithfield established itself as the largest meat market in England and the current market hall with its ironwork and glass roof was built to a design by Sir Horace Jones in 1868. Like most London markets it's only a shadow of its former self. As you pause to admire the ironwork at the entrance to Grand Avenue, you can now see the next pub on our route across to the right. This is the **Butcher's Hook & Cleaver** 2, a modern Fuller's bank conversion from 1999 with either a rather tacky or 'fun' name depending on your point of view. It has a cheerful interior with decent modern fittings and a spiral staircase leading to the comfortable mezzanine. The Fuller's beers are reliable, as evidenced by the pub's entry in the *Good Beer Guide*, but if you're only here for the architecture you can safely skip this one.

Before moving on from Smithfield, a brief detour to look at what remains of the splendid church of St Bartholomew the Great is recommended. Entry is via a passage just beyond Cloth Fair, the street by the Butcher's Hook. The Priory church was founded in 1123 as part of a monastery of Augustinian Canons, but was dissolved in 1539 and the nave of the church demolished. What remain are the impressive chancel, parts of the transepts and one side of the cloisters. The interior must surely be the most atmospheric of all London's parish churches.

Fortified spiritually, we can now walk down the narrow and attractive Cloth Fair, where the poet John Betjeman used to live, before we encounter the **Hand & Shears** 3 on a corner site. This has a very straightforward interior and is a significant Central London survivor of what is basically a Victorian layout. The woodwork is plain and simple and remarkably, there are still three separate bar areas plus a small snug partitioned off by simple screenwork. The plain floorboards and wooden panelling are entirely in keeping with this delightfully simple former working-

man's pub. Beers are from Courage and Theakston.

Cross the road and go through the archway by the old *Red Cow* into Hayne Street opposite. Emerge by Charterhouse Square and cross the road to walk along the left of the square, maybe detouring again to look at the enticing group of buildings on its northern side. This Oxbridge-looking building is Charterhouse, founded as a Carthusian monastery in 1370. The monastery was rebuilt as a private mansion in the Tudor period and, although the public school with which the name is perhaps associated most closely moved out to Surrey in 1872, the building still functions as an almshouse. Guided tours are available on Wednesdays only. Call 020 7253 9503 for details.

Returning to the task in hand, head through the gate at the north-western corner of the square to emerge at the **Fox & Anchor** 4. This 1898 reconstruction has a striking Art Nouveau exterior, including some fine Doulton tiling, executed by WJ Neatby, the artist responsible for Harrod's Food Hall. Inside is a long bar space which still retains some of the original partitions towards the rear.

The small central bar in the **Hand & Shears**

Beyond these you will find some small panelled rooms which feel very atmospheric even though they are later reconstructions. This is one of those pubs that opens very early for breakfast given that it is so close to Smithfield Market, although be aware that it may well close mid evening. Beers usually come from Adnams and Fuller's.

Just a little further down this narrow road we rejoin Charterhouse Street at a busy junction where the striking exterior of the **Hope 5**, with its curved windows and glazing bars, attracts the eye. Again, if you're an

early bird you can call in for breakfast from 7am, although if it's beer you're after you will have to wait until they've re-opened at 11am. A fairly small one-room interior awaits you behind the entrance, although there is an upstairs restaurant as well. A former Young's house, it still offers their bitter alongside Greene King IPA.

Consulting your map, find and walk up St John's Lane, the middle of three streets running north from the junction, and then turn left into Albion Place. A right turn at the end will lead you along Britton Street to last pub in this walk, the little **Jerusalem Tavern 6**. The name comes from the Priory of St John of Jerusalem, founded in 1140, which once stood in St John's Lane, but the building itself has only been a pub for about a decade. It was built in 1719–20 by Simon Mitchell, originally as a merchant's house. The interior, reached via a lobby room, has lots of atmosphere, and displays some eighteenth century panelling. Note also the 'four seasons' tile panels from the same period in the front lobby. The other noteworthy thing here is the beer, it's from the St Peter's Brewery of Suffolk whose fine ales are dispensed from wall casks.

It is a short walk back down Britton Street and right into Benjamin Street, which will bring you to Farringdon Station. **[LINK]**

Link Walk 23, **Mount Pleasant** (*page 103*). Continue up Britton Street turning left onto the Clerkenwell Road, where the first turn right brings you to Clerkenwell Green just short of the *Sekforde Arms* to join the start of the trail.

PUB INFORMATION for walk 18 Around Smithfield

1 Olde Mitre
1 Ely Court, Ely Place, EC1
020 7405 4751
11–11 Mon–Fri
Closed Saturday & Sunday
CAMRA National Inventory

2 Butcher's Hook & Cleaver
61–63 West Smithfield, EC1
020 7600 9181
11–11 Mon–Fri
Closed Saturdays
12–6 Sun

3 Hand & Shears
1 Middle Street, EC1
020 7600 0257
11–9 Mon–Fri
Closed Saturday & Sunday
CAMRA National Inventory

4 Fox & Anchor
115 Charterhouse Street, EC1
020 7253 5075
7am–8(or 9)pm Mon–Fri
Closed Saturday & Sunday
CAMRA Regional Inventory

5 Hope
94 Cowcross Street, EC1
020 7250 1442
7am–10am, 11am–8pm Mon–Fri
Closed Saturday & Sunday

6 Jerusalem Tavern
55 Britton Street, EC1
020 7490 4281
11–11 Mon–Fri
Closed Saturday & Sunday

WALK 19 **Islington**

WALK INFORMATION
Number of pubs: 6
Distance: 1¾ mile (2.75 km)
Key attractions: Islington Museum, Angel Gallery, Regent's Canal.
Beer range: ★★★
Pub architecture: ★/★★
Links: to walk 2

Islington is a district of London that has ridden the class rollercoaster from up to down and, in parts at least, back up again. It is a place of contrasts but it boasts a fine selection of handsome squares and terraces where gentrification has reached fever pitch. This walk takes us east of the centre into an area astride the Regent's Canal on a compact trail visiting some excellent hidden gems. Take plenty of money!

2 Charles Lamb

Start at Angel underground on the Northern Line, or bus it eastwards from Kings Cross/ St Pancras, and exit onto Islington High Street. The pubs here in the centre of Islington are best left to the crowds. None of them are particularly worthy of note, although if you want to try one, the *York* is probably as good as any. Walk north (to your right), and in a couple of minutes, close to the confusingly named Camden Passage market, turn right again at the *York* pub into Duncan Street. Head down to the end where ahead you will see the Regent's Canal exiting from a tunnel. Islington Tunnel, three quarters of a mile (about 1 km) long, was opened in 1819, a year before the canal itself. It cost £772,000 to build, which was twice the original estimate, and 120,000 tons of cargo were carried in its first year. A steam-chain tug was introduced in 1826 to reduce bottlenecks caused by boatmen manually 'legging' through it, and this service continued until the 1930s. You can walk down to the towpath here if you want to take a closer look, but otherwise turn right into Colebrooke Row and second

left at Elia Street to the **Prince Albert 1**. Modern refurbishments have gone down well with the discerning locals and this makes a nice retreat from the bustle of Upper Street. It hosts philosophy talks and jazz as well as offering an eclectic mix of books and magazines. Beerwise, expect to find a range of changing guest beers alongside M&B Brew XI and occasionally Mild. Please note that the pub lease was up for sale at the time of going to press.

It's a simple stroll to your next pub. Further along Elia Street turn left into Sudeley Street and at the far end you'll find the **Prince of Wales 2**. The place has been opened

The Regent's Canal near the **Prince of Wales**

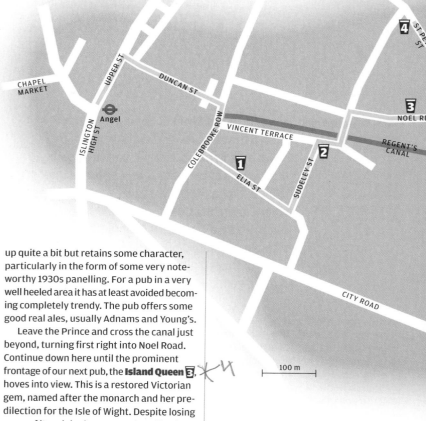

up quite a bit but retains some character, particularly in the form of some very noteworthy 1930s panelling. For a pub in a very well heeled area it has at least avoided becoming completely trendy. The pub offers some good real ales, usually Adnams and Young's.

Leave the Prince and cross the canal just beyond, turning first right into Noel Road. Continue down here until the prominent frontage of our next pub, the **Island Queen** 3, hoves into view. This is a restored Victorian gem, named after the monarch and her predilection for the Isle of Wight. Despite losing some of its original screenwork and having been modernised, it nonetheless retains its identity. The frontage still has three doorways and some impressive curved windows although sadly the glass is now all clear. Inside, the impression is one of space and grandeur around the central island bar area; note the slender and elegant stillion. To the left you can see how originally a porch would have led in from the door entrance; to the right, note the mosaic entrance. A separate room survives, divided by a nice screen but minus its door, and there is a corridor to the upstairs rooms. Etched glasswork by Morris of Kennington, who did the wonderful glass in the *Princess Louise*, High Holborn (see *Centre Point Horseshoe* trail, walk 10), survives

100 m

Exterior of the **Island Queen** and (*right*) screen inside

here and the dark lincrusta ceiling is another feature. The beers are good, with Fuller's London Pride and Timothy Taylor's Landlord usually served alongside a guest beer, while the extensive and interesting food menu reflects the affluence of the surroundings. Playwright Joe Orton lived at 25 Noel Road with his lover Kenneth Halliwell for the last few years of their lives, and was a regular in the Island Queen. It's ironic that the council has erected a blue plaque on his former abode as this was the same council which pressed for severe prison sentences against the two men, when they were found guilty of defacing local library books in 1962.

At the end of Noel Road, turn left into St Peter's Street and make your way up to the **Duke of Cambridge** 7, which is about 300 yards away. Claiming to be the world's first certified organic pub, the Duke of Cambridge was opened in December 1998 and has won several awards since, although the clientele's opinion seems divided, judging by some pithy comments on the internet. It certainly isn't cheap, either for food or drink. However, it's bright and modern, an interesting conversion of an old Victorian corner boozer. From a beer viewpoint the noteworthy thing is that they are all organic, coming from Pitfield and St Peter's breweries, so it's worth a visit on that account alone.

Walk back down St Peter's Street to the canal bridge and the **Narrow Boat** 5. Recently heavily modernised, only the outside reminds us of its Victorian past, and even that

REGENT'S CANAL

SHEPHERDESS WALK

WHARF RD

STURT ST

WENLOCK RD

Old Street

Inside the **Narrow Boat**

has been heavily painted. Inside it's Tardis-like with stripped floorboards, leather sofas and large sliding windows offering dramatic views over the canal below. In the summer the sliding windows are opened up to offer an experience not normally available to London pub-goers. Up to four real ales are on tap, mainly from the likes of Fuller's and Adnams.

If it is daylight and the canal towpath is open, come out of the pub onto the towpath and walk east. At the Packington Square/ Shepherdess Walk bridge, which is the next one, leave the canal and walk south down Shepherdess Walk. Take the first turning on the right into Sturt Street and walk to the end, where the **Wenlock Arms 6** stands on the corner. Alternatively, if you can't use the towpath, come out of the pub and walk

south down Wharf Road. Turn first left into Micawber Street and left again into Wenlock Road. Walk up the road and the Wenlock Arms is on the right.

The Wenlock will need no introduction to many CAMRA members, being a regular in the *Good Beer Guide* and a frequent winner of the Pub of the Year award from CAMRA's North London Branch. A traditional street-corner local, it has two regular beers (from Adnams and Pitfield) and at least three other guests, one of which is always a mild. There is also a range of imported beer and a real cider. Besides its solid support for the cause of good cask beer, it is also well known for its blues and jazz, usually on Friday and Saturday evenings. Unpretentious and good value food (carnivores should seriously consider the salt beef sandwiches) completes the happy scene and makes this a fitting finale to a worthwhile trail.

The Wenlock Brewery was once in this street, brewing from 1893 until 1962, when it was closed by Bass shortly after they acquired it. No trace now remains.

To return to civilisation in the form of public transport, walk down the Wenlock Road southwards (away from the canal) until you reach the main City Road in about 5 minutes. The nearest underground station is left along City Road at Old Street. **[LINK]** To return to Islington, walk to the right or catch a bus back to the Angel.

The **Wenlock Arms**

Link Walk 2, **Heart of the City** (*page 13*). Two stops southbound on the Underground from Old Street will drop you at Bank and the start of the trail.

PUB INFORMATION for walk 19 Islington

1 Prince Albert
16 Elia Street, N1
020 7837 5040
12–3; 5.30–11 Mon–Sat
12–3; 5.30–10.30 Sun

2 Prince of Wales
1a Sudeley Street, N1
020 7837 6173
11–11 Mon–Sat; 12–10.30 Sun
CAMRA Regional Inventory

3 Island Queen
87 Noel Road, N1
020 7704 7631
11–11 Mon–Sat; 12–10.30 Sun
CAMRA Regional Inventory

4 Duke of Cambridge
30 St Peter's Street, N1
020 7359 3066
12–11 Mon–Sat
12–10.30 Sun

5 Narrow Boat
119 St Peter's Street, N1
020 7288 0572
11am–midnight Mon–Sat
12–10.30 Sun

6 Wenlock Arms
26 Wenlock Road, N1
020 7608 3406
12–11 Mon–Sat
12–10.30 Sun

Southwark and the Borough

WALK INFORMATION
Number of pubs: 6
Distance: 1¾ mile (2.8 km)
Key attractions:
Southwark Cathedral,
Rose Theatre Exhibition,
Clink Prison Museum,
Borough Market.
Beer range: ★★★
Pub architecture: ★★/★★★
Links: to walk 24

Southwark, south of the original London Bridge and home to Borough Market, has a long history dating back to Roman times. Before the seventeenth century Puritan purges, and despite the land being owned by the Bishop of Winchester, it was a thriving red light district, illegally until 1611, when brothels were licensed by Royal decree. Thanks to the coming of the railway and the recent gentrification of the riverside, Southwark's character has changed considerably. There are some interesting pub buildings to savour and a treat too for beer lovers. In addition to Harveys only London tied house, there are two genuine free houses both with a very good range of beers from microbreweries, relatively rare in London.

Start at London Bridge station, and walk down the hill to Borough High Street, where the bulk of Southwark Cathedral competes with the railway bridges and viaducts for your attention. The Cathedral is probably more attractive inside than out, with the early English choir the most admired feature, while the nave is late Victorian. Turning left into the High Street, walk for a few minutes before coming upon the cobbled courtyard left, leading to the **George Inn** 🍺, London's only surviving galleried coaching inn. The George is only a vestige of its former self, as two sides of this old inn were demolished by the Great Northern Railway for warehousing about a century ago, and what remains is the south wing. This was not the first time it had been tampered with, as it was rebuilt in 1676 after a devastating fire swept through

Southwark. The room at the west end of the building as you enter the courtyard, is the real jewel, with panelling, fireplace and plain bench seating of considerable antiquity. Unfortunately though it is sometimes closed for private parties. Note the glazed servery with now rare examples of old fashioned 'cash register' style hand pumps. The ground floor rooms to the east were not originally pub rooms and have, along with the modern bar, been more recently brought into use. The panelled upstairs rooms are also well worth a look. Along with the house beer, George Ale, brewed by Adnams, there are usually offerings from the likes of Fuller's and Greene King.

Continue up Borough High Street for about five minutes until you reach St George the Martyr church and Borough underground station on the opposite side of the traffic lights. Follow Tabard Street which leads off to the *left* of the church, and then crosses the busy road, for your next quarry, the excellent **Royal Oak** ⧈. This pub will need no introduction to many readers, being CAMRA's London Pub of the Year in 2003. The Royal Oak is housed in a 1870s Victorian building, which was purchased and re-styled by Harveys of Lewes in 1997, and was their first London tied house. The style is robustly traditional, even down to the individual bars separated by a sort of pseudo off sales counter. As well as being a firm supporter of both CAMRA and of real ale, the pub serves all Harveys' seasonal ales as well as their regulars. At the time of writing, the site opposite is an enormous building site, no doubt soon to house a modern ugly development, so that is another reason to stay in this excellent pub. The food is recommended here too, with generous helpings and keen prices by London standards.

Leaving the Royal Oak, return to the traffic lights by Borough station and cross over to take the Marshalsea road running west, following this street as it curves gently right to meet the busy Southwark Bridge Road. Just before it does, the tiny Clennam Street runs off to the right, and you will see the next pub, the **Lord Clyde** ⧈ with its distinctive tiled exterior bearing the name of the former owners Truman Hanbury Buxton, and the erstwhile publican. This excellent local was rebuilt in 1913 and, unusually, retains two separate drinking areas, although there would have originally been more, as is apparent by the number of doorways. The main bar retains its tapering tongue-and-groove counter, bar back, an original fireplace and some of the original etched glass. The back room has a hatch to the servery. The Lord Clyde dates from a time of relative austerity as far as pub building is concerned, contrasting with the splendour of the late Victorian period before it. This is a real locals' pub, run by the same family for almost 50 years. Beers served include those from Fuller's, Adnams and Shepherd Neame.

Leaving the *Clyde*, rejoin Marshalsea Road and cross Southwark Bridge Road into the

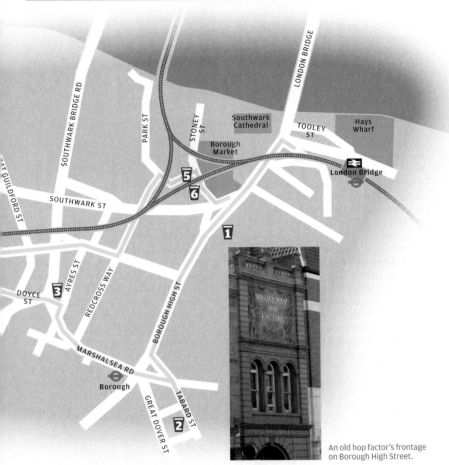

An old hop factor's frontage
on Borough High Street.

narrow Doyce Street opposite, pass a now
unusual admonition to 'Commit no nuisance',
and then a left plus a right turn takes you into
Copperfield Street, renamed to commemorate the Dickens character. The attractive
Winchester Cottages on the left were provided by the Church Commissioners and
inspired by social reformer Octavia Hill. The
small garden opposite occupies the site of
All Hallows Church, which was bombed in
the Second World War and is now the subject
of a bitter local development dispute. Take
Risborough Street, the second on the right,
bringing you directly to your next pub, the
appropriately named **Charles Dickens 4**.
Following a recent change of name and
management, this attractive pub looks set

to become an important addition to the real
ale scene south of the river. Up to six changing and well kept ales, many from microbreweries, are served in the pleasant traditional atmosphere of this free house. The
rear area is set aside primarily for food.

Follow Union Street eastwards, with the
railway viaduct on your left. If you wish to
break the trail with a visit to the celebrated
Tate Modern, turn left at Great Guildford
Street (see map; less than 10 minutes' walk).
Otherwise, cross back over Southwark Bridge
Road and turn left into Redcross Way towards
Borough Market. Turn right at the T-junction
at the end of the road and this leads straight
to the market at Stoney Street. The market
represented an obvious place for the fruit and

vegetable growers of Kent to sell their wares to London, standing as it does right next to the main road into the city, although these days it is changing, with several upmarket eateries competing with the fruit and vegetable stalls. Both pubs on this street are worth a visit, and the first is right on the corner here, the **Market Porter** 5. This is a pub that has had several ups and downs, but currently is popular with a varied clientèle. It's a lively place with an interesting and well-kept range of beers on the eight hand-pumps. The regular is Harvey's Sussex Bitter, and some unusual beers can be found here as well as established favourites. The interior, whilst much altered, still retains some character.

It's just a very short step along the road, directly under the railway viaduct to the **Wheatsheaf** 6. This is a simple, no-frills Victorian 'boozer', rebuilt in 1890 and now owned by Young's. Inside, the décor is about as unfussy as you get with worn floorboards, dark oak panels and simple furnishings. It retains its two rooms, the lettering on the

The **Wheatsheaf**

doors identifying 'Public Bar' on left and 'Saloon' on right. The two are in fact barely distinguishable, and separated by a plain wood panelled and glazed partition and a small serving area.   **[LINK]**

London Bridge station is a short walk away. Turn right at the end of Stoney Street to rejoin Borough High Street and you will recognise the spot where you started. Pause to look at the nice tiled exterior of the *Southwark Tavern*, with hop motifs that also appear on buildings across the street, reminding us of the old hop trade from Kent which is now sadly a shadow of its former size. The London Dungeon, Hays Wharf and the Riverside walk are just beyond the station, access in Tooley Street.

The **Market Porter**

Link Walk 24, Riverside (*page 109*). To join the trail, walk down Stoney Street beyond the *Market Porter* and at the T-junction turn right for the *Old Thameside Inn*, left for the *Anchor*.

PUB INFORMATION for walk 20 Southwark and the Borough

1 The George RA
77 Borough High Street, SE1
020 7407 2056
11–11 Mon–Sat
12–10.30 Sun
CAMRA National Inventory

2 Royal Oak RA
44 Tabard Street, Borough, SE1
020 7357 7173
11–11 Mon–Fri; Sat 6pm–11.30pm
Sun 12 noon–6.30pm

3 Lord Clyde RA
27 Clennam Street, SE1
020 7407 3397
11–11 Mon–Fri; 12–4; 8–11 Sat
12–4; 8–10.30 Sun
CAMRA Regional Inventory

4 Charles Dickens RA
160 Union Street, SE1
020 7401 3744
11.30am–11pm Mon–Sat
12–8/9pm Sun

5 Market Porter RA
9 Stoney Street, SE1
020 7407 2495
11–11 Mon–Sat
12–10.30 Sun

6 Wheatsheaf RA
6 Stoney Street, SE1
020 7407 7242
11–11 Mon–Fri; 12–8 Sat
Closed Sunday
CAMRA Regional Inventory

The Inner Western Suburbs: Notting Hill and Bayswater

WALK INFORMATION
Number of pubs: 6
Distance: 1⅞ mile (3 km)
Key attractions:
Kensington Gardens, Whiteley's Shopping Centre, Portobello Road Market, Hyde Park, Notting Hill shops.
Beer range: ★★/★★★
Pub architecture: ★★/★★★
Links: to walk 25

As late as the 1950s, Notting Hill was still described by some as a slum while the insalubrious bedsitters of the area, many of which were owned by notorious landlord Peter Rachman, became home to many West Indian migrants. The Pembridge Road area saw Britain's first race riots in 1958, in response to which the now celebrated Notting Hill Carnival was born. Today, things are rather different, and this is a good pub tour to do if you have come into some money, although to be fair this compact walk actually takes us around the posher south-eastern side of Notting Hill, touching Kensington and Bayswater. Like most of the routes in this book you will probably see more if you can do the walk during the day.

🏃 **Start at Notting Hill underground** station and exit onto the southern side of the road. It's little more than a five-minute walk east along to the junction with Kensington Church Street, and down to the **Churchill Arms** 🍺 on the corner of Campden Street. One of the things the Victorians were very good at in their pubs was creating a homely intimacy, which was down to a combination of dark colours and clever use of space. The Churchill is one of those pubs that has this sense of warmth, and feels welcoming as soon as you walk through the door. Large enough to cater for the wide range of customers who appreciate it, this pub has a bit of everything. There is good beer from Fuller's, who have owned the Churchill since 1973, and several drinking areas despite much opening out of the interior. The well-regarded food, with

Thai dishes a speciality, is served in an atmospheric rear conservatory. The latter is actually a former yard, which has a glass roof with dozens of pot plants creating a jungle-like canopy. A splendid little rear

The handsome exterior of the **Churchill Arms**

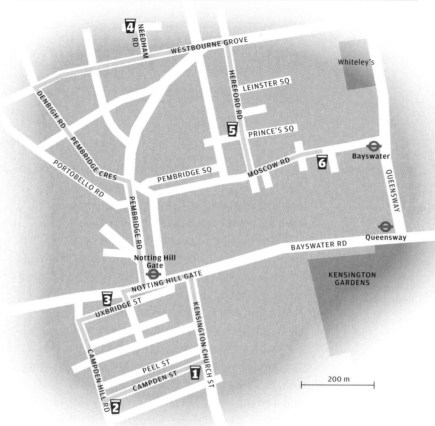

room just before the conservatory is also used for dining. However, if you wish to eat here it may be advisable to book ahead.

Over the years, the place has amassed a sizeable collection of bric-a-brac such as jugs, lamps, chamber pots and newspaper cuttings. You certainly won't get bored here. Snob screens survive on the bar counter although they do look a little like beached whales; to see some in their true context try the *Bunch of Grapes* on the Hyde Park trail, walk 25, or the *Lamb*, Bloomsbury, walk 23. The Churchill is a very good pub and one you won't want to leave. Nonetheless, at some point leave you must, and the next pub is worth the short walk.

Stroll up Campden Street and, at the top end, turn right and there it is. The **Windsor Castle** 7, like the Churchill, was refitted in the 1930s, but the heavily divided interior

layout is more typically Victorian. Here you can admire timber panelling, screens and some curious doorways between the separate rooms, which were probably inserted for cleaners (compare with the *Prince Alfred* in Maida Vale, walk 7, page 35). New rooms have also been added to the drinking area with very little loss of character. If and when you have had your fill of the interior there is a garden too. The beer range is also enticing with Fuller's London Pride, Timothy Taylor Landlord and two guests, often from micro-brewers. If you can get here at a quiet time, you can walk around and admire the different rooms at your leisure. You can eat here too.

Walk down Campden Hill Road, back towards Notting Hill, and take the last turning before the traffic lights at the junction with the main road. Here in a secluded back street, just behind the mayhem of Notting

Service door and exterior (*top*) at the **Windsor Castle**

Hill Gate, is our next pub, the attractive **Uxbridge Arms** 5. Largely unknown and therefore neglected by the hordes of trippers making their way north to the market, this is very much a traditional locals' pub. It's very comfortably furnished and serves a reliable pint, which usually includes beer from Fuller's, Young's and Greene King. You can sit outside in good weather, as this is a quiet street.

Carry on along Uxbridge Street and take the next left, Hillgate Street, which quickly brings you out close to the underground station. It's a wee stroll to our next pub so you may wish to fortify yourselves in one of the sandwich bars of Notting Hill Gate. Another diversion that pub architecture devotees may wish to consider at this point is a short bus trip to the *Elgin Arms*, 96 Ladbroke Grove, with its superb mirror and screenwork. Take the useful and frequent No 52 bus, alighting by the pub just one stop before Ladbroke Grove station. Return the same way. Either way, head up Pembridge Road, north from the main junction. Take the right-hand option in a few yards and a couple of turns left beyond Portobello Road, home of the well-known market, turn down Chepstow Crescent. At the second crossroads, by a converted church, turn right into Westbourne Grove. Now turn left into Needham Road and, at the end of this short street, on the corner, is the **Cock & Bottle** **4**. Of early Victorian origin, this pub is now very smart but traces of its former multi-room layout remain, alongside some snob screens, although these are modern. The jewel here though, is the splendid bar back with its unusual shape and remarkably ornate detailing. The nice little illuminated stained glass panels with the swan motifs, commemorating the pub's former name, are probably interwar. Beers such as Draught Bass, Greene King IPA and Fuller's London Pride are on offer, along with lunch-time food.

Return to Westbourne Grove and continue east, taking the second right into Hereford Road, which puts us firmly in Bayswater with its hotels and general air of affluence. Just past Leinster Square, and still on Hereford Road, we arrive at our next port of call, the spacious **Prince Edward** **5**, on the right. Considering the location, and the fact that tourists from nearby hotels make up a good deal of its trade, the pub is pleasantly unpretentious and comfortable. The drinking area is arranged around an island bar. There is some etched glass worth looking at and well-kept beers come from the likes of Fuller's

and Marston's, which have made it a frequent entrant in the Good Beer Guide. Food is available at most hours.

Suitably fortified, it's an easy walk to our last pub. Continue down Hereford Road to Moscow Road, turn left and a five-minute stroll brings us to the **King's Head** **6**. This is a nice, relatively unspoilt pub. It is opened out but still has a traditional feel. Note the three sets of doorways suggesting the former partitions. Floorboards and dark panelling give it a sense of gravitas. The other draw here is the ambitious beer range, with Fuller's London Pride, Young's Bitter and up to five guest beers. You can eat in here until 9pm. Look out for the interesting old brewery adverts on the walls.

With Bayswater underground just at the end of Moscow Road, it's nice to know that transport is close at hand at the end of a punishing pub walk! Before you dive down, however, you may either wish to eat (Chinese food is a speciality here), or take a look at Whiteley's shopping centre. This was originally the first and biggest department store in the country and may have even attracted the admiration of Adolf Hitler who, according to some stories, ordered the Luftwaffe not to bomb it as he fancied it as his headquarters once he'd conquered Britain. Whiteley's closed in 1981 but the name lives on in the modern shopperama. **[LINK]**

Link Walk 25, Hyde Park (page 115). To join the trail, walk down Queensway to the Bayswater Road, and either take a bus heading east, or if it's fine, cross the road and stroll along in Kensington Gardens as far as Lancaster Gate to pick up the early pubs. Check the map and route details.

PUB INFORMATION for walk 21 **Notting Hill and Bayswater**

1 Churchill Arms	**3 Uxbridge Arms**	**5 Prince Edward**
119 Kensington Church Street, W8	13 Uxbridge Street, W8	73 Princes Square, W2
020 7727 4242	020 7727 7326	020 7727 2221
11–11 Mon–Sat; 12–10.30 Sun	12–11 Mon–Sat	11–11 Mon–Sat
CAMRA Regional Inventory	12–10.30 Sun	12–10.30 Sun
2 Windsor Castle	**4 Cock & Bottle**	**6 King's Head**
114 Campden Hill Road, W8	17 Needham Road, W11	33 Moscow Road, W2
020 7243 9551	020 7229 1550	020 7229 4233
12–11 Mon–Sat; 12–10.30 Sun	12–11 Mon–Sat; 12–10.30 Sun	11–11 Mon–Sat
CAMRA National Inventory	CAMRA Regional Inventory	12–10.30 Sun

WALK INFORMATION
Number of pubs: 7
Distance: 3.2 miles (5 km)
Key attractions:
Richmond Park,
Royal Botanic Gardens
Kew, Ham House,
Thames Path.
Beer range: ★★
Pub architecture: ★
Links: to walk 27

Richmond is one of London's most elegant suburbs and occupies an enviable position between the city's largest open space and one of the loveliest reaches of the river. Once a favoured royal residence, Sheen Palace (Sheen is Old English for 'beauty spot') was rebuilt under Henry VII and renamed Richmond, after his earldom in Yorkshire. Oliver Cromwell destroyed most of it after 1649 although some buildings remain close to our route. We also take in the sedate backwater of Richmond Green, a good stretch of the riverside, the famous view from the top of Richmond Hill, now a World Heritage site, and some of the area's attractive residential streets.

🏃 **Richmond station** is accessible by fast and frequent trains from London Waterloo and Clapham Junction. Upon exit cross the road and turn right, making your way past the *Orange Tree* pub to the big roundabout just beyond. Here, use the traffic lights to cross the Twickenham Road, and head down the short alley ahead marked 'residents only' leading to a terrace of houses. Bearing left here, walk down via another short alley to reach our first pub. The **Triple Crown** 🍺, which has a rugby ground opposite and the Old Deer Park beyond, was once the *Tulip Tree* according to its front elevation, and sits in a quiet lane. Inside, a comfortable but narrow drinking space runs along the single bar counter and a good range of beers is available, including Timothy Taylor Best Bitter, Woodforde's Wherry and Fuller's London Pride. There is an outside drinking area for good weather.

The **Triple Crown**

Moving on, head left along the lane back up to the busy road, following it down to your right to cross by the footbridge about 250 yards further along. Then follow 'town centre' signs on a path leading at right angles from the bridge, bear right to traverse the edge of a car park and swing left to cross the railway on another foot bridge. We emerge in a far more attractive environment on the northern side of Richmond Green. This open space was originally a common where villagers pastured their sheep, but later on it became a medieval jousting ground alongside Richmond Palace. It's now a haven of tranquillity very close to the centre of town and bordered by attractive, mostly Georgian houses. Walk around the green to the right keeping it on your left, and turn right again to follow Old Palace Road at the end, despite the 'No through road' sign. This charming old street, as the name suggests, was close to the Old Palace, though only the gatehouse and parts of the old wardrobe in the courtyard survive from the Tudor palace built by Henry VII. It was a royal residence from 1125 until 1688, and Elizabeth I died here in 1603. Beyond the charming little terraced cottages lies our next pub, the **White Swan** ☑. This old building has been given the gastro treatment and the inside has been heavily modernised and opened out, although the location is very agreeable. The pub offers three real ales, typically Fuller's London Pride, Old Speckled Hen and Wells Bombardier. There is a nice rear garden as well. An interesting feature of this establishment is the freestanding pub sign about 100 yards away on the riverside

further down the lane. What a pity that the art of painting attractive pub signs seems to have died out! At least we can admire the attractive brickwork on the railway viaduct on the way. The Thames Path here is a popular route. Follow it upstream past the remains of the Palace towards Richmond Bridge, just before which, right on the riverside is your next pub, the well-known **White Cross** ☑. The name stems from the site of a convent built by Henry VII in 1499, with the white cross being the friars' insignia. There has been a pub here at least since 1780 although the present building dates from 1835. It's a very spacious but popular building and at certain times you might find it difficult to get a seat. Like many riverside pubs you have to climb steps to gain entry as the river around regularly floods. Note the unusual fireplace with a window above. Young's has long owned this pub, so expect their beers.

Just up from the White Cross on the narrow lane is another well-known Young's house. This is the **Waterman's Arms** ☑, which started life as a simple beerhouse, originally named the *King's Head*. The interior of the Waterman's still retains much of its divided layout, though it is yet another pub that has succumbed to the Thai food revolution.

Returning back down Water Lane to the river, and continuing along the Thames Path, we pass the Georgian-style offices on our left and go under Richmond Bridge. At this point, if you cannot face the steep climb further ahead, you could omit the next pub, the **Roebuck** ☑, simply by climbing up to the road, taking the path into the town, turning right and bearing left to reach the Victoria (see map). However, the Roebuck has the finest view in the book so don't forsake it lightly. Follow the river path for about another half a mile to a point where, just before a sharp turn to the right and close to public toilets, a path forks left to join the road. Then, across the road, a steep straight path climbs up the hillside towards a terrace of buildings on Richmond Hill. Here, overlooking that famous view of the Thames as it sweeps below you, stands the Roebuck.

Inside there still remain vestiges of a compartmentalised layout, and the interior

Cottages adjacent to the **White Swan**

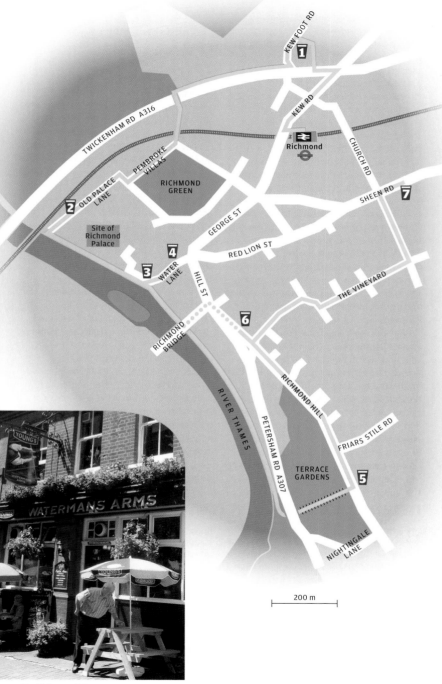

KEW FOOT RD

1

KEW RD

TWICKENHAM RD A316

Richmond

CHURCH RD

PEMBROKE VILLAS

OLD PALACE LANE

RICHMOND GREEN

SHEEN RD

7

2

Site of Richmond Palace

GEORGE ST

RED LION ST

4

WATER LANE

THE VINEYARD

3

HILL ST

6

RICHMOND BRIDGE

RIVER THAMES

RICHMOND HILL

FRIARS STILE RD

PETERSHAM RD A307

TERRACE GARDENS

5

NIGHTINGALE LANE

200 m

WATERMANS ARMS

YOUNGS

The **Waterman's Arms**

is dark and panelled with several nooks and crannies. There are three regularly changing beers available and food is served at lunchtimes and evenings. In good weather you can take your beer across the road and sit on the pleasant terrace to enjoy the World Heritage river view at its best. You should be able to pick out several landmarks, from the roof of Ham House close to the river below you, to the massive stadium at Twickenham across the river further right.

Leaving the Roebuck, continue down Richmond Hill back towards the town centre. After a few minutes, just as the lower and upper roads are about to merge, lies the next pub on the walk, the **Victoria** [6]. This must be one of the smallest pubs in the book, and is pleasantly unpretentious. In the single room with comfortable seats and benches, three beers are served from Wells, Young's, and Adnams. In good weather you can sit in the rear courtyard. Appropriately for such a small pub, food is confined to snacks and sandwiches.

We now have a short walk down the attractive residential back streets of Richmond to reach our next pub. Walk back up the road for about 25 yards and turn left into The Vineyard, pass the church and follow this road for about half a mile to reach a T-junction at Church Road. Turn down here to the left and at the traffic lights our next pub, the **Red Cow** [7], is merely 50 yards to the right. This is another Young's house that has been given a makeover to align it with Richmond's affluent populace. You may or may not like the outcome, but the beer quality is very

The tiny **Victoria Inn**

reliable and it's a regular entry in the *Good Beer Guide*. The corner site of this pub means that there is plenty of light in the drinking area surrounding the central island bar.

It is a very short walk back to Richmond station. Return to the traffic lights and turn right to continue along Church Road. Just beyond the railway bridge an alleyway leads us back to the station.   [LINK]

Link Walk 27, **Isleworth to Kew** (*page 123*). Take the Underground or Silverlink one stop to Kew Gardens, and thence you can reverse the trail from the *Inn at Kew Gardens*.

PUB INFORMATION for walk 22 **Richmond**

[1] Triple Crown
15 Kew Foot Road, Richmond,
Surrey   020 8940 3805
11–11 Mon–Sat; 12–10.30 Sun

[2] White Swan
26 Old Palace Lane, Richmond,
Surrey   020 8940 0959
11–11 Mon–Sat; 12–10.30 Sun

[3] White Cross
Riverside, Water Lane, Richmond,
Surrey   020 8940 6844
11–11 Mon–Sat; 12–10.30 Sun

[4] Waterman's Arms
10 Water Lane, Richmond,
Surrey   020 8940 2893
11–11 Mon–Sat; 12–10.30 Sun

[5] Roebuck
130 Richmond Hill, Richmond,
Surrey   020 8948 2329
11–11 Mon–Sat; 12–3; 7–10.30 Sun

[6] Victoria Inn
78 Hill Rise, Richmond, Surrey
020 8940 2531
11–11 Mon–Sat; 12–3, 7–10.30 Sun

[7] Red Cow
59 Sheen Road, Richmond,
Surrey   020 8940 2511
11–11 Mon–Sat; 12–10.30 Sun

WALK 23 **Tour de Mount Pleasant**

WALK INFORMATION

Number of pubs: 8
Distance: 1¾ miles (2.7 km)
Key attractions: Charles Dickens Museum, Karl Marx Memorial Library, British Museum, Old Clerkenwell village St James's church, Spa Fields and Exmouth market.
Beer range: ★★
Pub architecture: ★★
Links: to walk 8

This seems like as good a name as any for a saunter through the no-man's land straddling WC1 and EC1. Between Bloomsbury to the west and Clerkenwell/Finsbury to the east, it traces an arc around the Post Office's huge sorting office at Mount Pleasant, close to the Gray's Inn Road. There are no fewer than eight pubs on our walk, and with six of them open at weekends, this route is a good option for a leisurely Saturday or Sunday.

Start at Farringdon, on both the Thameslink line and the Underground, and turn left and left again, out of the station, to follow the tracks north along Turnmill Street. Cross Clerkenwell Road into Farringdon Lane and then go right into Clerkenwell Green. Clerkenwell takes its name from the Clerk's Well in Farringdon Lane. Once a small village retreat, it was transformed by the Industrial Revolution and became a centre for breweries, the printing industry and clock and watchmaking. Many former industrial buildings here have now been converted into expensive loft dwellings.

Clerkenwell Green is at the centre of the old village, by St James's church. As we walk past the attractive frontage of the *Crown* and look up to the church we can get an impression of what is one of the better preserved village centres in inner London. Isaak Walton lived here while he wrote the *Compleat Angler*, as did Karl Marx, whose Memorial Library is at No. 37a.

Keep going beyond the *Crown*; take the next left into Sekforde Street, and noting

the attractive terrace on the left, walk down to the **Sekforde Arms** 1. The Sekforde is also to be admired, being a solid traditional pub in this up-and-coming district. Owned by Young's, it's a pub with only one room but is cheerful and functional.

Moving on, take the road northwards, into Woodbridge Road. Again, there is a splendid terrace, with an unusual but faithfully reproduced new section in the centre of the street: maybe this was a replacement for bomb damage? At the end turn left into Skinner Street, keeping the open space, Spa Fields, on your left. These existed as pleasure gardens from the seventeenth century onwards, although with bull-baiting and other nefarious activities taking place here, theatregoers to nearby Sadler's Wells paid to be escorted through the area. Spa Fields was also the site of a notorious burial ground, with about 8,000 bodies being buried in the tiny space in the early nineteenth century. It was converted to a public garden in 1886. Follow the traffic and the white lines along the winding road for a short distance past

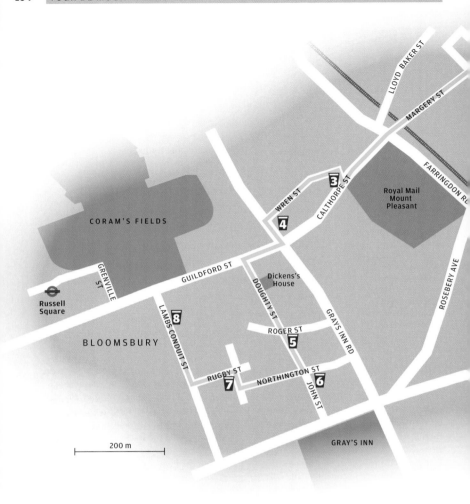

the garden, when it becomes Tysoe Street and leads us, at the junction with Rosebery Avenue, to the **Old China Hand 2**. Exmouth Market with its interesting shops and eateries is just off to the left before the junction.

The new owners who took this free house over last summer seem determined to promote the place as an outlet for microbreweries, and you can expect to find up to four ales from the likes of Oakham, O'Hanlon's and Sharp's. The genuine dim sum available at lunchtimes and evenings in the no smoking eatery upstairs is an interesting variant on

the usual Thai food. Jazz is on the menu too on Wednesday evenings. The pub was a great favourite in its former *O'Hanlon's* heyday and, although some regret the sprucing-up of the back room and the presence of plasma TV screens, it's still an atmospheric place with some tasteful oriental wooden furniture. During good weather there are tables and chairs for outdoor drinking.

Turn right on leaving the pub, and head up past Wilmington Square, keeping the green on your left, then turn left at Margery Street. Lovers of interesting architecture

scene of Arnold Bennett's novel *Riceyman's Steps*, on the right.

At the bottom of Margery Street, at Farringdon Road, cross into Calthorpe Street, with views of the Post Office headquarters over to the left, and your next port of call, the **Pakenham Arms** 3, is a few yards ahead. Mount Pleasant is the country's largest sorting office and about a third of all inland mail in Britain comes through here. It's no surprise then that the Pakenham is the posties' local. Because of this, it's open from 9am to 1am every day so you should be able to get a drink here however early or late you are running! If you arrive at busy times, or when sport is on the big TVs, it may be distracting, but it's spacious and cheery with a patio and seats at the front. Above ground floor level it's a handsome building in dark red brick with stone quoins and window arches. Fuller's London Pride, plus beers from Adnams and Harveys are usually available, often joined by changing guest beers. Food is available for much of the day.

The next stop is very close by. Take Wren Street, which runs down the left side of the pub on exit, and walk down to the end. Here, at the junction with Gray's Inn Road, is the excellent **Calthorpe Arms** 4. A fine Young's house in a Victorian building with an attractive brick and tile corner frontage, the Calthorpe is a traditional local which has the accolade of being the local CAMRA Pub of the Year in 2001 and 2004. It made a small piece of history back in 1830, when it was used as a temporary magistrates' court after the first recorded murder of a policeman on duty. It is usually a fairly quiet pub with a TV that is rarely obtrusive. Food is available, the upstairs dining room is open at lunchtimes and outside seating is available in a pavement patio area.

Upon leaving the Calthorpe, cross into Guilford Street opposite and take the first left into Doughty Street. The Charles Dickens Museum is along here on the left. When the great author moved here in 1837 it must have been on the very northern fringe of the city. Dickens lived here for only two years but wrote *Nicholas Nickleby* and *Oliver Twist* during this time. It's the only one of some

may wish to make a short detour at this point. Head straight across Margery Street and take the little alley at the end of the short road through to Lloyd Baker Street. This interesting estate of extraordinary and very handsome individual houses was laid out by Thomas Lloyd Baker in the 1820s. You can walk northwards towards Great Percy Street but return to Lloyd Baker Street and join the trail by heading downhill here (west) to Farringdon Road, where the end of Margery Street is only a few yards on the left. En route, be sure to look at Granville Square, fifteen London addresses he had to have survived intact. Beyond, on the same side of the road at the junction with Roger Street, lies further refreshment, in the shape of the **Duke of York 5**. Lovers of 1930s architecture will drool over this largely intact survivor from that period, complete with those horrid metal-framed windows at first and second floor level. Inside it retains its two bars and much has survived down to the Art Deco flooring, the doors, and the wall panelling. It's a real period piece, a rare survivor from

this time, and possibly the best of its kind in Central London. Adnams and Greene King IPA are the ales you can expect to find here, along with food.

The prominent **King's Arms 6** can be found on the corner of John Street, further down the continuation of Doughty Street. It is worth a look if it's open, though it is closed at weekends. This is a largish one-bar pub with a pleasing mosaic in the Northington Street entrance. Here one can sit and admire the Georgian streetscape outside. Beers are

The very distinctive thirties entrance to the **Duke of York**

Window detail and interior (*below*) of the **Duke of York**

Draught Bass, Greene King IPA and a regular guest.

We now head west along Northington Street, turning right from John Street, and right again at the end into Great James Street (note the blue plaque commemorating author Dorothy L Sayers). Here, the large and handsome frontage of the **Rugby Tavern** 7 is visible. Formerly a Nicholson's and later a Fuller's house, it is now owned by Shepherd Neame and serves their beers. If you have time and stamina and it isn't the weekend, this *Good Beer Guide* regular is worth a visit, though not at the expense of our last pub. Food is reasonably priced and recommended, and the semi-pedestrianised street gives this location the feel of a quiet backwater. If the tables are outside and the sun is shining you may find a stop hard to resist.

Swing round to the left out of the Rugby Tavern into Rugby Street and turn right into Lamb's Conduit Street, named after the six-teenth century philanthropist William Lamb who improved the water supply to this area by the construction of a new conduit. On the left, we pass the *Perseverance* pub, perhaps the first pub in London to offer a wide range of independent brewery beers, back in the late 1970s, when it was known as *The Sun*. Further up on the right-hand side is arguably Bloomsbury's best pub, the **Lamb** 8.

From the urbane exterior with its tiled, glass and brick elevation over which hangs a pendant lantern, right down to the interior ambience, this pub gets most things right and strongly evokes the character of a bygone era. A pub was first recorded here in 1729, although what we have today is largely a Victorian rebuilding of an earlier structure. This was one of the few pubs in London to retain some snob screens *in situ*. These small pivoting panels of etched glass on the bar counter were positioned at head height to increase privacy, which was an important consideration in the Victorian pub. Here they look at their best, far more realistic than in some places where they no longer serve any practical function. The Lamb, serving the range of Young's beers, is a regular in the *Good Beer Guide* and there is food available. All in all, this is an excellent finale to the trail. From here, it's a short walk to Russell Square underground station. Go to the top of the road and turn left. Take the second right and go into Grenville Street, and then turn left into Bernard Street. The station is about 200 yards along on the left. **[LINK]**

Link Walk 8, **Legal London** (*page 37*). For an even longer trail, walk straight down Lamb's Conduit Street via Red Lion Street to High Holborn, then left to reach the *Cittie of York* and reverse the trail.

The elegant front elevation of the **Lamb**

Snob screens at the **Lamb**

PUB INFORMATION for walk 23 **Tour de Mount Pleasant**

1 Sekforde Arms
34 Sekforde Street, EC1
020 7250 3385
11-11 Mon-Fri; 12-4 Sat-Sun

2 Old China Hand
8 Tysoe Street, EC1
020 7278 7630
11-midnight Mon-Thurs
11am-2am Fri-Sat; 12-10.30 Sun

3 Pakenham Arms
1 Pakenham Street, WC1
020 7837 6933
9am-12.30am Mon-Sat
9am-10.30pm Sun

4 Calthorpe Arms
252 Gray's Inn Road, WC1
020 7278 4732
11-11 Mon-Sat; 12-10.30 Sun

5 Duke of York
7 Roger Street, WC1
020 7242 7230
12-11 Mon-Sat; 12-10.30 Sun
CAMRA National Inventory

6 King's Arms
11a Northington Street, WC1
020 7405 9107
11-11 Mon-Fri
Closed Saturday and Sunday

7 Rugby Tavern
19 Great James Street, WC1
020 7405 1384
11-11 Mon-Fri
Closed Saturday and Sunday

8 Lamb
94 Lamb's Conduit Street, WC1
020 7405 0713
11-11 Mon-Sat
12-4; 7-10.30 Sun
CAMRA Regional Inventory

WALK 24 **Riverside: Waterloo to Tower Bridge**

WALK INFORMATION

Number of pubs: 9
Distance: 2⅜ miles (3.75 km)
Key attractions: South Bank complex, London Eye, London Aquarium, Tate Modern, Millennium bridge, Shakespeare's Globe Theatre, Borough Market, Southwark Cathedral, *HMS Belfast*, The Tower of London, Tower Bridge.
Beer range: ★★/★★★
Pub architecture: ★
Links: to walk 20

This long walk takes in the best of London's excellent Thames Path, including some stretches that were previously inaccessible. Views are very good, with many major landmarks to be seen. However, due to the huge growth in the popularity of the South Bank and the riverside in general, you are advised to go at quieter times if you want to enjoy the riverside pubs at their best. With no less then nine pubs in this trail, you can safely skip any you don't like the look of.

Start at Waterloo station (National Rail and Underground), and make your way out of the main entrance close to the Eurostar terminal, down the impressive steps, and look out for your first pub. Underneath the arches of the Charing Cross to Waterloo East railway in front of you, you'll spot the sign for the **Hole in the Wall** 🛈. This pub is something of an institution. Even though the façade is no architectural gem, inside there remains a real atmosphere which derives in large part from its unique location, as the trains thunder overhead. Meanwhile, the wooden benches and chairs, and the unpretentious, even shabby, décor give the place a sort of beer hall ambience. There is a small front room which is a little more upmarket than the more atmospheric and larger rear room, where an array of handpumps dispense up to six (pricey) beers, including the tasty, locally brewed Battersea Bitter. Food is available from a counter in the rear room. This is a good place to kick off a pub trail, though it can get very busy when large sports fixtures are on. Non-smokers beware: it can get very smoky at times.

Unfortunate name change caused by rampant vegetation

Exit the pub and turn left under the rail arch with the classical façade of St John the Evangelist church (1822–4) ahead of you across the road. Cross by the lights and walk down Exton Street until you come to the junction with Cornwall Road. Directly across is Roupell Street, a quasi-Victorian scene of terraced houses that would be worth a visit even without the pub to come. The houses here display a rare unity as their sash windows

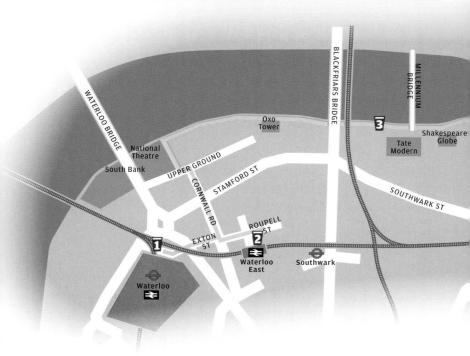

and simple doors have been pretty much kept intact, with no tacky modern replacements in sight. Halfway along, the elegant **King's Arms** 2 fits perfectly into this scene. The pub hasn't made too many concessions to its new affluent clientele, but it's no dingy Victorian den either. Two bars are separated by a screen, and out at the rear, a yard has been pleasingly converted into a conservatory where you can sit and eat at rustic old tables, whilst admiring the eclectic assemblage of knick-knacks on the wall. Beers come from Adnams, Fuller's and Young's.

Heading off in search of the river, retrace your steps down Roupell Street still admiring these lovely old cottages, which were probably built for a few pounds and are now worth a king's ransom, and turn right into Cornwall Road at the end. Go past the *White Hart*, itself not a bad pub, and cross Stamford Street down to the T-junction at the end. Here, by the vile IBM office block you'll see a signpost to the Thames Path some 30 yards to the left. Head down this alley with the 1960s

The **King's Arms**

National Theatre on your left, to reach the river close to the new Hungerford footbridge. Walk east along the wide promenade past the OXO Tower and Sea Containers House, and continue under Blackfriars road and rail bridges. The builders of the OXO Tower got round a ban on advertising by designing the windows in the shape of the letters of the famous stock cubes! Public access is possible up to and including the eighth floor viewing terrace. Just beyond the bridges sits another modern pub. This is the Young's-owned **Founders Arms** 3. Opened in 1980 and

occupying an enviable riverside position, the pub doesn't have a great deal of atmosphere as is often the case with places whose clientele is almost completely transient, but many like its bright and modern layout, so feel free to make up your own mind. The beer quality is reliable though and you can sit on the terrace and watch the river go by. It's a very busy pub, with the opening of the nearby Tate Modern and the new Millennium Bridge putting a lot of pressure on the staff which can often affect service. One other thing, it opens for breakfast at 9am.

The pub sign outside the **Founders Arms** looking out across the Thames to St Paul's Cathedral

The Tate Modern is the acclaimed reincarnation of the old Bankside Power Station, which was opened in 1947 and designed by Sir Giles Gilbert Scott, who was also the architect of Battersea Power Station, the massive Anglican cathedral in Liverpool and the famous British red telephone box. The station closed in 1981 but has been a roaring success since reopening as the Tate Modern in May 2000. The next highlight on this very touristy stretch is the reconstructed Shakespeare's Globe Theatre, after which we pass under Southwark Bridge and arrive at the rambling **Anchor** 4. This is the heavily altered and much extended tap of the old Barclay Perkins Anchor Brewery, which in the middle of the nineteenth century was the largest of its kind in the world, covering over 12 acres on either side of Park Street. It was from the Anchor that Samuel Pepys witnessed the destruction of the Great Fire of London in 1666. I doubt he would recognise it now though, as the additions have rather overwhelmed it. Although there is some character left, particularly in the little corner room named after another patron, Dr Johnson, the predominant feeling is one of insensitive modernisation. The pub suffers by being thronged with tourists and pre-theatre visitors: the riverside area in front of the pub has been extended, crammed with garden furniture and patio heaters. The beer is Courage, plus a guest, and of course there is food if you want it.

Continue along the riverside under the rail bridge into an area that has had the tourist treatment big time in recent years. For a start, the once infamous Clink Prison now advertises corporate hospitality! [LINK]

At the end of the street by the replica of Drake's *Golden Hind* is another pub you may wish to try, the **Old Thameside Inn** 5. Despite the name, this was actually a spice warehouse until 1985 and, even though it is a magnet for tourists, the good river views and reasonable beer are worth a stop. The beer is usually Fuller's London Pride.

Continuing along the Thames Path, which leads us around the northern side of Southwark Cathedral and under London Bridge, we rejoin the river in the area of Hay's Wharf. Just beyond the Hay's Galleria covered shopping mall, which is a conversion of the Old Hay's Dock, is our next pub, the **Horniman at Hays** 6. This is a former warehouse with a spacious interior surrounding an attractive servery where beers from the likes of Fuller's and Tetley are available, as well as guests. If the weather is fine, you can sit on the terrace outside by the river and admire HMS *Belfast*, which is moored close by.

Walk back through the Galleria to rejoin Tooley Street and the next pub is visible across the road. This is the **Shipwrights Arms 7**, an imposing Victorian building on a corner site. Don't miss the splendid tiled picture just inside the left hand door. There are few of these left in London pubs these days, and this one, naturally, has a nautical theme. Note also the island bar, a late Victorian development to maximise the efficiency of the serving area. There are three well-kept real ales on tap here, usually from some of the bigger brewers.

Go back across the road and follow the pedestrian alleyway with a curious little rivulet running down the middle of it, which leads us to the riverside in the vicinity of the new City Hall. The riverside at this point has been opened out to give fine views of

Tower Bridge. The pedestrian path leads under the Bridge towards another area of rejuvenated warehouses, which this time have retained more of their character during the restoration. It's worth walking a little way down Shad Thames, the much filmed and atmospheric narrow street which runs between the towering warehouses of Butler's Wharf. However, sightseeing done, go down Horselydown Lane, which runs away from the river just under Tower Bridge, and past the *Anchor Tap* which despite an attractive, traditional appearance does not serve real ale. At the top of the street bear right to join Tower Bridge Road, and just to the left at the traffic lights is the **Pommeler's Rest 8**. This is a typically spacious Wetherspoon's pub, but unusually for pubs owned by the chain, it's not always packed, and is also

The exterior of the **Shipwrights Arms** and detail (*right*) of the carving above the entrance

Old warehouses on Shad Thames near the **Pommeler's Rest**

completely non-smoking. It's a conversion of what was formerly The *Tower Bridge Hotel*, and, although congenial enough, somehow the splendour and gravitas of the old building do not really come through that strongly – a shame, given Wetherspoon's good record for pub conversions. You can enjoy the usual wide selection of beers, many from small breweries, which one has come to expect from this chain, and food is available pretty much all day.

The last port of call on this marathon walk is a short stroll back up towards the Bridge from the Pommeler's. The **Bridge House** 9 is an unusual beast for London in that it is tied to the Suffolk brewery Adnams. So, whilst it's common to find their beers all over London, this pub has pretty much the whole range on offer, in a modern cafe bar atmosphere.

There are no underground stations close to the Bridge House, so your best bet is to take a bus, either the useful RV1 towards London Bridge or, crossing the road, buses 42 or 78 towards Liverpool Street if you're heading north or east.

LINK Walk 20, Southwark & Borough (*page 91*). Leave the riverside after the Anchor by heading up Stoney Street (unnamed but next right, with a rail arch visible) to meet the *Market Porter* and *Wheatsheaf* a couple of minutes later.

PUB INFORMATION for walk 24 Riverside: Waterloo to Tower Bridge

1 Hole in the Wall
5 Mepham Street, SE1
020 7928 6196
11-11 Mon–Sat; 12-10.30 Sun

2 King's Arms
25 Roupell Street, SE1
020 7207 0784
11-11 Mon–Sat; 12-10.30 Sun

3 Founders Arms
52 Hopton Street, SE1
020 7928 1899
9am–11pm Mon–Sat
12-10.30 Sun

4 Anchor
34 Bankside, SE1
020 7407 1577
11-11 Mon–Sat; 12-10.30 Sun

5 Old Thameside Inn
Pickfords Wharf,
Clink Street, SE1
020 7403 4243
11-11 Mon–Sat; 12-10.30 Sun

6 Horniman at Hays
Unit 26, Hay's Galleria,
Counter Street, SE1
020 7407 1991
11-11 Mon–Sat; 12-10.30 Sun

7 Shipwrights Arms
88 Tooley Street, SE1
020 7378 1486
11-11 Mon–Sat; 12-10.30 Sun
CAMRA Regional Inventory

8 Pommeler's Rest
196-8 Tower Bridge Road, SE1
020 7378 1399
10-11pm Mon–Sat; 12-10.30 Sun

9 Bridge House
218 Tower Bridge Road, SE1
020 7407 5818
11.30-11 Mon–Sat; 12-10.30 Sun

WALK 25 **Across Hyde Park: Paddington to Knightsbridge**

WALK INFORMATION
Number of pubs: 5
Distance: 2½ miles (4.1 km)
Key attractions: Hyde Park, Victoria & Albert Museum, Harrods, Natural History Museum, Science Museum, Brompton Oratory.
Beer range: ★★
Pub architecture: ★★★
Links: to walk 12

This is a very good trail boasting some top-notch pubs, all of architectural interest, with an attractive interlude taking in Kensington Gardens and Hyde Park along the Serpentine. What's more, if you don't fancy spending the rest of the day in Harrods, you can drink your way right down to Victoria by linking up with the Belgravia trail. What are you waiting for?

Start this trail at Paddington main line and underground station and emerge via the main exit onto Praed Street. Look for London Road, which leads off at the left-hand corner of the station, and saunter down past the parade of shops, by which time you may see a stern picture of our longest serving monarch staring lugubriously at you in the distance. She might have been cheered by the pub which takes her name, however, for the **Victoria 1**, at the corner of Strathearn Place, is a splendid survivor from the middle years of her reign. Internally, the real treasure here is the glass and mirror work, especially the gilded glass set in the wonderful bar back and screen on the back wall. The interior décor also gets it right with smart floorboards and a variety of comfortable seating areas. Do not miss a trip upstairs to see both the modern but agreeable ambience of the Theatre Bar, and the very impressive Library Room with its leather seats and an atmosphere redolent of a gentlemen's club. The beers are from Fuller's, and a varied food menu is served throughout the day. All in all this is just the sort of place to set you up for an enjoyable day.

Reluctantly leave the Victoria and head off down Stanhope Terrace opposite, turning

The Theatre Bar in the **Victoria**

right to skirt round the northern side of Sussex Square. Don't miss the blue plaque on a modern house just round the corner facing the square, marking the site of one of Winston Churchill's homes. You should be able to make out the next pub, as its sign is visible along the street as you turn around the top side of the square. The **Archery Tavern 2** in Bathurst Street is an agreeable little early Victorian pub, owned by Hall & Woodhouse and serving their beers. Comfortably furnished throughout and with lots of dark panelling, it has the unusual distinction for London of lying next to working stables. Sitting in the

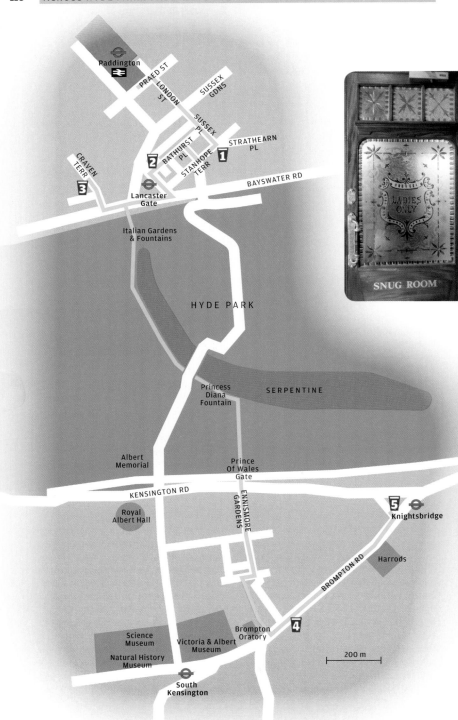

Paddington

PRAED ST

LONDON ST

SUSSEX GDNS

SUSSEX PL

STRATHEARN PL

BATHURST PL

STANHOPE TERR

CRAVEN TERR

2

1

3

BAYSWATER RD

Lancaster Gate

Italian Gardens & Fountains

HYDE PARK

Princess Diana Fountain

SERPENTINE

Albert Memorial

Prince Of Wales Gate

KENSINGTON RD

ENNISMORE GARDENS

Royal Albert Hall

5

Knightsbridge

BROMPTON RD

Harrods

Science Museum

Victoria & Albert Museum

Brompton Oratory

4

Natural History Museum

200 m

South Kensington

LADIES ONLY

SNUG ROOM

back room listening to the hooves trotting down the passage outside, one could almost feel transported to the countryside. Although it is opened out to some degree it still retains the intimacy that the Victorians liked in their pubs. Sadly, the future of this pub is uncertain, so please ring before visiting.

At the end of Bathurst Street you come upon a very busy racetrack, so cross by the lights into Lancaster Terrace, keeping the massive Lancaster Gate Hotel on your left to reach the Bayswater Road in 200 yards. Turn right here with views of Kensington Gardens across the road. Pass the *Swan*, which looks nice but is more of a restaurant these days, and turn first right into Lancaster Gate which immediately becomes Craven Terrace. In no time you will find the tall and striking **Mitre** **3** occupying a prominent corner site with a mews to the left. Again the sparkling etched glasswork is the star of the

The **Mitre**'s handsome exterior and etched glass (*top left*)

show, not least in and off the corridor on the right-hand side, which leads down to what was formerly a billiards room. There is some surviving tile-work and a little snug leading off, with 'ladies only' on the door. The main room has plenty of character although it is hardly original. Don't miss also the mosaic in the corridor, or the attractive little porch on the street angle entrance. This free house offers Hogs Back T.E.A. along with more familiar beers and lunchtime food.

We now have a chance to get some exercise, though if you really can't face a short walk through the Park, go from Lancaster Gate to Knightsbridge by tube, and pick up the trail at the Paxton's Head (see below). Otherwise, drop back down to the Bayswater Road, and cross by the lights near the *Swan* to enter Kensington Gardens, which can be enjoyed as you take the path to the right of the fountains and ponds. Follow this very attractive waterside route along past the Peter Pan sculpture and there is a good spot for a siesta not far beyond here. This upper section of the Serpentine is the prettiest part of the long lake, created by damming the tiny West-bourne River in 1730. The path ducks under the road bridge and past the (in)famous Lady Diana memorial 'fountain'. For a fool-proof exit from Hyde Park, take the path immediately before the Lido café beyond the bridge, and walking at right angles away from the lake you will spot the two Italianate gatehouses that lead out of the Park via the Prince of Wales Gate. As you stroll across the grass, reflect that on this spot a huge glass building known as the Crystal Palace was assembled for the Great Exhibition in 1851, before being dismantled and carted off to a windswept spot in South London which later bore its name.

The road opposite is Ennismore Gardens. Walk down here, noting the very fine square towards the bottom lined with graceful houses. At the foot of the road, before turning right to locate a footpath alongside the public garden, pause to look left to the next corner where an interesting mews pub, the *Ennismore Arms* stood until recently. Its absence is a reminder that our pub heritage is continually subject to pressure. Walk down the path alongside the garden of Holy Trinity church into the quiet Cottage Place. The imposing building on your right is the Roman Catholic Brompton Oratory, one of London's finest churches and certainly among the most flamboyant. It is closely modelled on the Gesu Church in Rome and if you are sober and suitably attired, I thoroughly recommend a visit. Beyond, if you are so inclined, is the V&A Museum.

Turning left onto the Brompton Road, away from the Oratory, the next quarry, the **Bunch of Grapes** 4, soon appears across the road. Take a moment to admire the elegant early Victorian elevation before crossing the road to enter this well-preserved pub. On no account omit to look at the lovely back-painted mirrors on the wall, or indeed the array of snob screens, which are among the best-preserved in London. The dignified interior is well endowed with dark woodwork and the bulky carved 'bunch of grapes' partition is particularly noteworthy. The beers are Young's Bitter and Fuller's London Pride.

Snob screens and carved panel in the **Bunch of Grapes**

Continue walking up the Brompton Road, past or via Harrods, crossing the road back to the north side. Just before the main road junction there is a little alleyway that leads through to Knightsbridge and almost directly to our last pub, the **Paxton's Head** 5. Don't worry if you can't find the alleyway, simply double back left at the corner. Rebuilt at the turn of the last century, here again you can enjoy some splendid glasswork on the walls and doors around the large mahogany island bar. At one time there would have been several compartments but these, almost inevitably, have gone. Downstairs there is an atmospheric little bar, and upstairs, via a lobby, a pan-Asian restaurant. Beers usually come from the likes of Charles Wells, Fuller's and Adnams. Incidentally, the head celebrated in the pub's name is that of Joseph Paxton, the nineteenth century designer of the Crystal Palace and the Tropical House at Kew Gardens. As mentioned earlier, the Palace was originally erected nearby, and it has been suggested that workers frequented this place, and gave the pub its name, although this seems to be merely conjecture. Interestingly the use of this site for a pub goes back many generations and has survived the wholesale Edwardian redevelopment of the block.

Knightsbridge underground station is but a stone's throw away, as are buses, notably the frequent 52 for Victoria. [LINK]

LINK Walk 12, Belgravia (*page 59*). To join the trail, walk east along Knightsbridge, crossing the two main roads, and in a few minutes you'll see Wilton Place on the right. Turn down here, and at the first crossroads is the traverse between the *Grenadier* (left) and the *Nags Head* (right, see maps).

PUB INFORMATION for walk 25 Across Hyde Park: Paddington to Knightsbridge

1 Victoria
10a Strathearn Place, W2
020 7724 1191
11-11 Mon-Sat; 12-10.30 Sun
CAMRA Regional Inventory

2 Archery Tavern
4 Bathurst Street, W2
020 7402 4916
11-11 Mon-Sat; 12-10.30 Sun

3 Mitre
24 Craven Terrace, W2
020 7262 5240
11-11 Mon-Sat; 12-10.30 Sun
CAMRA Regional Inventory

4 Bunch of Grapes
207 Brompton Road, SW3
020 7589 4944
11-11 Mon-Sat; 12-10.30 Sun
CAMRA Regional Inventory

5 Paxton's Head
153 Knightsbridge, SW3
020 7589 9932
11-11 Mon-Sat
12-10.30 Sun
CAMRA Regional Inventory
(mirrorwork, right, in the Paxton's Head)

Chiswick and Turnham Green

WALK INFORMATION
Number of pubs: 7
Distance: 2¾ miles (4.5 km)
Key attractions:
Fuller's Brewery,
William Hogarth's House,
Chiswick House, Bedford
Park Model Village.
Beer range: ★
Pub architecture: ★★
Links: to walk 17

Another fine walk with much architectural interest. This is a pleasant saunter through the home territory of Fuller's, one of London's two large family brewers. In fact, the brewery towards the end of this walk is close to the original riverside settlement of Chiswick, while the modern Chiswick, along the High Road, is more properly Turnham Green, best known for a 'battle' on its Common in 1642, when the Royalist march on London under Prince Rupert was halted. Culture vultures will enjoy Hogarth's House and nearby Chiswick House and grounds.

🏃 **Start by taking the underground** (District Line) to Chiswick Park station. Failing this, Gunnersbury on Silverlink and the District Line is a short bus ride away to the west. Chiswick Park is one of several underground stations designed by noted architect Charles Holden in the early 1930s and is now listed. Its distinctive circular shape was ahead of its time and sets a nice tone for the walk to come. From the station, walk south down Acton Lane to join the Chiswick High Road right by our first pub of the day, the impressive **Old Pack Horse** 🍺.

Work by Nowell Parr at the **Old Pack Horse**

This is one of several pubs in the area designed by architect Thomas Henry Nowell Parr, who worked on it in 1910 for Fuller's, to replace an earlier building they had acquired in 1849. His trademark was his use of distinctive Tudor archways. The pub's attractive frontage conceals an interior that has lost its partitions but still retains several

Chiswick Park Underground station, classic Charles Holden

119

separate drinking areas. Perhaps the most attractive is the old saloon on Acton Lane with its fine entrance porch, attractive alcove with fireplace and a handsome bar back with inset clock. See if you can spot the remains of the off-sales corridor evident between the saloon and the former public bar. Fuller's beers, which you will get used to on this walk, are on tap.

Walking eastwards along the Chiswick High Road it is not long before we reach our next pub, the **Crown & Anchor** ②. Recently reopened by a private company after being sold by Young's, this listed building's exterior with its distinctive tile-work dates back to a major alteration in 1936. The plethora of doorways suggests a formerly heavily divided interior, although today we find a smart upmarket internal layout in which a couple of very nice Art Nouveau fireplaces have survived. Expect a good range of beers from some of the larger brewers.

Cross the Chiswick High Road and continue walking eastwards to reach the large and imposing frontage of the **George IV** ③, which was acquired by Fuller's in 1848. The current building is a smartened-up 1930s pub with a food menu, serving the range of Fuller's beers, alongside occasional guests. The handsome exterior of this big pub is complemented by a pleasing internal layout with nice small screens and panelling as well as a partially tiled floor.

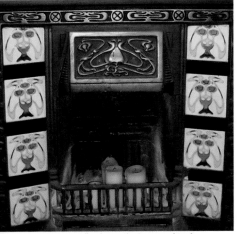

Art Nouveau fireplace at the **Crown and Anchor**

Cross back to the north side of the road and walk to the left at the traffic lights and then just a little further along, past the shops of Turnham Green Terrace and under the railway bridge. Here, just to the right sits the architectural highlight of this walk, the **Tabard** ④. This is no ordinary pub, having been designed by architect Norman Shaw to serve the model village of Bedford Park in 1880. The Park was created as a middle-class commuting village in the 1880s, inspired by the industrial model villages like Bournville. It soon became a community of writers, artists and other bohemians and to get a flavour of the residential estate, walk just beyond the Tabard and take the first left into Priory Gardens. The rest of this considerable building was formerly a stores serving the estate. The Tabard was restored in 1971 and, in line with Bedford Park's artistic origins, now includes a theatre. The interior of this Grade II* listed building is still a delight, even though there has been some opening out. Don't miss the fine original tiles by William De Morgan in the entrance and in the bars; and further ones by the artist Walter Crane around the fireplace to the left of the bar, in a style that was a precursor of Art Nouveau. There's a wide range of beers available, along with a food menu.

Retrace your steps back down to the traffic lights on the Chiswick High Road, turn right, cross the road again and take Devonshire Road, the next turning on the left. This pleasant residential street, which runs down towards the notorious Hogarth roundabout, is home to two pubs almost opposite each other. We are interested in the pub on the right, the **Duke of York** ⑤, which has been part of Fuller's estate since 1834. Recently added to CAMRA's Regional Inventory, this mid-1920s building, which sits on the site of an older pub, is another Nowell Parr work with his distinctive Tudor arches in evidence. Much of the original work survives, including the bar back, bar counters and one original stained glass screen between two seating alcoves. Three hand pumps dispense a range of well-kept ales from Fuller's, whose brewery is just down the road.

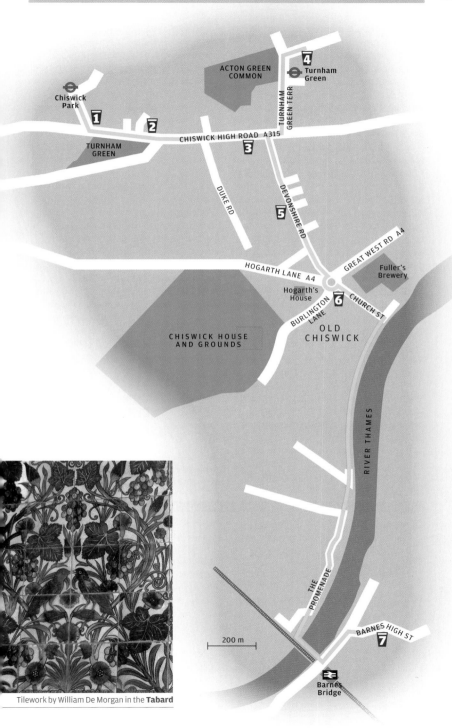

ACTON GREEN
COMMON

Turnham
Green

Chiswick
Park

TURNHAM
GREEN TERR

TURNHAM
GREEN

CHISWICK HIGH ROAD A315

DUKE RD

DEVONSHIRE RD

GREAT WEST RD A4

HOGARTH LANE A4

Fuller's
Brewery

Hogarth's
House

CHURCH ST

BURLINGTON
LANE

CHISWICK HOUSE
AND GROUNDS

OLD
CHISWICK

RIVER THAMES

THE
PROMENADE

BARNES HIGH ST

200 m

Barnes
Bridge

Tilework by William De Morgan in the **Tabard**

As we continue down Devonshire Road, architecture enthusiasts may wish to peer in at the *Devonshire House* across the street which retains some very fine work by Nowell Parr, although sadly there is no real ale. Upon reaching the end of Devonshire Road, with Fuller's Brewery beckoning you, take the subway which leads under the nightmarish Hogarth roundabout, otherwise you may not even reach your next pub which is at the subway exit, doing its very best to stand aloof from the traffic. The **George & Devonshire** 6 is one of Chiswick village's oldest pubs, and sits at the northern end of the charming old village street, or at least what survived after being truncated by the A4 and the roundabout. Unsurprisingly, the present building is a twentieth century rebuild and equally predictably serves beers from Fuller's brewery which towers over the pub from across the street. It retains its two-bar layout, and I would recommend the nicely panelled and unpretentious public bar. Food is available lunchtimes and evenings.

If you have had enough at this point, be warned that the nearest rail stations are a fair way off. Your best bet is the 190 bus, south (same side as the pub) towards Richmond for good rail links to London Waterloo and Clapham Junction, and northwards back to Chiswick for the underground (District Line). [LINK]

If you are still game for a beer but don't fancy the 'official' continuation to Barnes along the river (below), no more than 200 yards west and tucked adjacent to the brewery site itself, is the *Fox and Hounds and Mawsons Arms*, which has been the Fuller's brewery tap since the turn of the last century.

However, for the more energetic, there's the small matter of a walk of just a little over a mile via the Thames Path down to Barnes for a final drink before catching the train. Walk down the pleasant little Church Street adjacent to the George and Devonshire; this is the kernel of the original settlement of Chiswick. Upon reaching the river, take the Thames Path heading upstream, by some modern flats. The first 200 yards or so take us along a semi-privatised riverside past a modern housing development, but then the path skirts an open space before Barnes Bridge comes into view with the old village visible on the other side of the river. Cross the bridge alongside the railway line and walk back up the road for about 100 yards before turning right by the *Bull's Head* to find the more intimate **Coach & Horses** 7, a Young's house in the High Street. This attractive little pub with its cobbled yard, award winning garden and vestiges of a multi-room layout is a pleasant way to end the trail. It also leaves us very close to Barnes Bridge station for frequent trains back to London Waterloo.

LINK Walk 17, Hammersmith (*page 79*). A pleasant riverside walk leads to this trail, less than half a mile away. Walk down Church Road and bear left along the riverside path in Chiswick Mall to meet the trail at the *Black Lion*.

PUB INFORMATION for walk 26 **Chiswick and Turnham Green**

1 Old Pack Horse
434 Chiswick High Road, W4
020 8994 2872
11–11 Mon–Sat
12–10.30 Sun
CAMRA Regional Inventory

2 Crown & Anchor
374 Chiswick High Road, W4
020 8995 2607
11–11 Mon–Sat
12–10.30 Sun

3 George IV
185 Chiswick High Road, W4
020 8994 4624
11.30–11 Mon–Thu
11.30am–midnight Fri–Sat
12–10.30 Sun

4 Tabard
2 Bath Road, W4
020 8994 3492
12–11 Mon–Sat
12–10.30 Sun
CAMRA Regional Inventory

5 Duke of York
107 Devonshire Road, W4
020 8994 2118
12–11 Mon–Sat; 12–10.30 Sun
CAMRA Regional Inventory

6 George & Devonshire
8 Burlington Lane, W4
020 8994 1859
11.30–11 Mon–Sat; 12–10.30 Sun

7 Coach & Horses (Barnes)
27 Barnes High Street, SW13
020 8876 2695
11.30–11 Mon–Sat; 12–10.30 Sun

WALK 27 Thames Riverside, Isleworth to Kew

WALK INFORMATION
Number of pubs: 8
Distance: North route 3½ miles (5.75 km); South route 4 miles (6.5 km)
Key attractions:
Kew Botanic Gardens, Kew Steam Museum, Osterley Park, Syon Park House, gardens and Butterfly House.
Beer range: ★★/★★★
Pub architecture: ★★
Links: to walks 22 and 26

This is a varied walk which can be shortened or extended, taking you through old Isleworth village, one of the more unspoilt parts of London's riverside, and across Syon Park to Brentford. Here you rejoin and follow the river to Kew Bridge, taking either the northern route to finish at the traffic-free riverside of Strand-on-the-Green, or following the southern route across to Kew itself with the option to visit the world-renowned Botanic Gardens. A shorter version of this trail omitting Isleworth and Syon Park and starting at Brentford is also possible: see the end of this walk for details.

This is a train trip, so start at Waterloo or Clapham Junction and take the frequent South West Trains service to Isleworth (35 minutes from Waterloo). Come out of the main entrance of the station, turn right, and right again into Linkfield Road under the rail bridge. Our first pub, the **Red Lion** 🛈, is a few minutes down on the left, and was the local CAMRA branch Pub of the Year in 2003 and 2004. A huge rambling building with an eclectic partly-tiled exterior, it has two large rooms each with a range of drinking areas. This free house offers Young's bitter and a wide range of changing, often interesting, guest beers. There always seems to be something happening here, including beer festivals. This is a good pub to kick off any trail.

Leaving the Red Lion, continue down to the end of Linkfield Road, which will take about 10 minutes. Turn right onto the main road, and almost immediately turn left by the river bridge into the ancient route of Mill Plat, which is now a pedestrian alleyway.

A quiet corner in the **Red Lion** Isleworth

Entrance (*top*) and bar at the **Red Lion** Isleworth

Pass the Ingram Almshouses, a terrace of six homes built in 1664 by Sir Thomas Ingram, erstwhile Chancellor of the Duchy of Lancaster, and emerge by the site of the old mill alongside the Thames in old Isleworth village. Go left here through the old village street down to the **London Apprentice 2**. This large and attractive Georgian pub takes its name from the City livery company (or trade association) apprentices, who occasionally rowed up on their days off and stopped here for refreshments. The interior subdivisions have gone (look out for the double doorways on the road side) and there is an increasing emphasis upon food, but the riverside setting is a charming place in which to drink beer from the likes of Fuller's and Courage. Look out for the old etched glass advertising Isleworth ales, from the Isleworth Brewery, which was bought by Watneys in 1923. Being popular it can get very busy at peak times. Across the road is the handsome tower of Isleworth church, which is flanked with incongruous modern buildings thanks to the actions of a group of schoolboys who burnt the rest of it down in 1943!

THE LONDON APPRENTICE

Double doorway and old etched glass (*below right*) at the **London Apprentice**

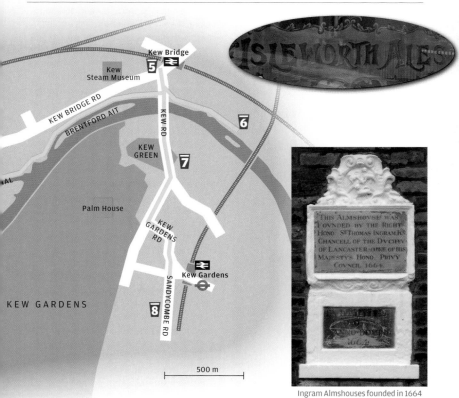

Ingram Almshouses founded in 1664

Just along the riverside past the church the Thames Path is well signposted as it turns right into Syon Park. Originally the site of a medieval abbey, Syon House and its 200-acre park is the London home of the Duke of Northumberland whose family has owned it for 400 years. Walk up the roadway past the fascinating Butterfly House and through the park, keeping to the cycle route through the car park and house precincts if you feel you are about to lose your way. The Thames Path then emerges on the busy A315 road just west of Brentford High Street. Turn right, pass two or three pubs and the Grand Union Canal bridge, before reaching your next port of call, the **Magpie & Crown** 🖪, which is tucked back off the street frontage. A *Good Beer Guide* regular, this is an excellent pub and a great supporter of microbreweries. There are usually four regularly changing beers on tap and it is a great source of pride to the pub that over 1,500 different beers

have been sold here since 1996. In addition to the real ales, the pub sells foreign beers, some on draught, plus cider and perry. Devotees of pub history should be able to discern some of the pre-existing layout from what is now a one-bar pub. The old public bar was formerly on the right-hand side, off-sales were straight in front upon entry and there were also two former rooms on the left, marked by separate doorways and a slight change of floor level.

Continue east along the High Street for a short while, and before the traffic lights and the Fuller's-owned *Beehive* (opposite) turn right down Catherine Wheel Road. Just when you think you have strayed in error upon a tormented landscape of commercial premises, you come unexpectedly upon a nice little pub right by the Grand Union Canal and the river, the **Brewery Tap** 🖪. This is yet another Fuller's house, whose name refers to a long defunct victim of a takeover, and it still retains some vestige of its former multi-roomed layout. It's a real community local which combines good beer with a varied food menu, plus plenty of events, especially music. The steps up to the door are a reminder that the vicinity can be prone to flooding.

Upon exit from the pub, a narrow path opposite leads across a creek to the Grand Union Canal. However, our acquaintance with the canal is brief, for we need to climb back up to the bridge in front of us. Don't take the Thames Path at the bridge: otherwise you will end up in Hanwell. Instead, turn left onto the cobbled street which brings you back to the dismal main road by the supermarket. The Thames Path here turns right and drops back to the river, finally emerging at Kew Bridge. Follow the signs carefully. Alternatively you could take the bus – no-one will know!

Across the road ahead, right on the busy interchange is the **Express Tavern** 🖪. Here, you'll find well-kept beers in a tastefully decorated pub. Although greatly remodelled, its past character persists. There are three interlinked rooms, with the rear room, not originally part of the public drinking area, being particularly handsome, with its 1930s features. It leads to a pleasant garden, but please keep off the grass. A framed award

The **Magpie & Crown** Brentford

on the wall commemorates the founding of the local branches of CAMRA in this pub in 1974. It has seen very frequent appearances in the *Good Beer Guide* since. Beers come from Young's alongside Draught Bass, with the latter long established here (note the dinky pump clip), and there are usually up to two guest beers as well. Food is only available at lunchtimes. Be aware that the Express closes in the afternoon, so if you arrive during the interregnum it's best to go ahead to the other pubs on this walk, and return here later.

Upon leaving the Express we have a choice. If you are full up, the rail station at Kew Bridge is almost adjacent. If you wish to continue, the trail now splits in two, and you can choose either the northern or southern option, or both if you are in for the duration.

Northern route

Cross the wide and busy road to get to the opposite side of the bridge approach, and then drop down the slip road to regain the riverside. Five minutes' walk brings us to the old hamlet of Strand-on-the-Green. Just beyond the point where the road and path diverge lies the **Bell & Crown** 6. Beerwise, this old smugglers' haunt is the best bet of the three riverside pubs along this pleasant traffic-free vista. This is another long-standing Fuller's pub, boasting a couple of conservatories and an outdoor patio. It makes the most of its' location, but it can get thronged with visitors, not to mention locals from the pleasant but unbelieveably expensive houses nearby. Food is also available all day in this *Good Beer Guide* regular. Opposite the pub is

A promising sign – window at the entrance to the **Brewery Tap** Catherine Wheel Road

the tiny Oliver's Island, named for Cromwell who, legend has it, took refuge here during the Civil War and used the pubs on the bank.

Further along the riverside promenade, close to the rail bridge, there are the *City Barge* and *Bull's Head*. However, if you want more real ale I would recommend a return to Kew Bridge to take the southern route. On the other hand, if you have had enough, return to Kew Bridge Station.

Southern route

From the Express Tavern, cross the bridge and walk down the main road to the south side of Kew Green. This is the centre of the old village, but is now riven in two by the nasty South Circular road. Here, set back a little from the road, is the **Coach & Horses** 7, an upmarket Young's hotel. Inside, there's a spacious L-shaped bar, traditionally panelled, with an adjacent room on the left, set aside as a restaurant with fish specialities. Outside there is a large garden. This is another *Good Beer Guide* regular where you can rely on the ales.

To finish this long but hopefully rewarding trail, turn left out of the Coach & Horses and stroll up Kew Road on the right at the traffic lights, with the wall of Kew Gardens opposite. At the next set of lights turn left, and follow the road round to the right, past the line of trendy cafés and boutiques leading to Kew Gardens station, by which time you will see the last port of call, the **Inn at Kew Gardens** 8. Formerly the *Kew Gardens Hotel*, this was acquired by the Capital Pub Company late in 2004 and has been taken firmly upmarket. Nonetheless, despite an emphasis on food and wine, there are six handpumps and a good variety of well-kept beers from some of the larger brewers. The handsome exterior with its columned entrance portico is complemented by a bright and spacious interior that says aspiring 'gastro-pub', a statement backed up by the presence of sofas and the odd three-wheeled buggy in the bar area. Food is reasonably priced given the opulence of the neighbouring residential area, and it is worth a visit. Afterwards, return to Kew Gardens station for fast services to Clapham Junction and London via Richmond, as well as the useful North London Line to Stratford.   **[LINK]**

A shorter version of this trail, omitting the first two pubs and the walk through Syon Park, may appeal. Alight at Brentford station, two stops before Isleworth, and walk down the main road southwards to the main Brentford High Street by the *Beehive*, an attractive Fuller's house that would make a good alternative opener. Then turn right and walk along the High Street for five minutes to reach the Magpie & Crown (above).

LINKS Walk 22, **Richmond** (*page 99*), is the nearest from Kew Gardens. Take the train back to Richmond as above, but if you are at Kew Bridge station, however, take a 65 or 391 bus into Richmond. Another attractive option from here is to take the 391 the other way (or the 237 and 267), and a short journey brings you to **Chiswick**, and the Old Pack Horse at the start of **Walk 26**.

PUB INFORMATION for walk 27 **Thames Riverside, Isleworth to Kew**

1 Red Lion
92-94 Linkfield Road,
Isleworth, Middx.
020 8560 1457
11-11 Mon-Sat; 12-10.30 Sun

2 London Apprentice
62 Church Street,
Isleworth, Middx.
020 8560 1915
11-11 Mon-Sat; 12-10.30 Sun

3 Magpie & Crown
128 High Street, Brentford, Middx.
020 8560 5658
11-11 Mon-Sat; 12-10.30 Sun

4 Brewery Tap
47 Catherine Wheel Road,
Brentford, Middx.
020 8560 5200
11-11 Mon-Sat
12-10.30 Sun

5 Express Tavern
56 Kew Bridge Road,
Brentford, Middx.
020 8560 8484
11.30-3; 5.30 (6 Sat)-11
12-10.30 Sun
CAMRA Regional Inventory

6 Bell & Crown
11-13 Thames Road,
Strand on the Green, W4
020 8994 4164
11-11 Mon-Sat; 12-10.30 Sun

7 Coach & Horses Hotel
8 Kew Green, Kew, Surrey
020 8940 1208
11-11 Mon-Sat; 12-10.30 Sun

8 Inn at Kew Gardens
292 Sandycombe Lane,
Richmond, Surrey
020 8940 2220
12-11.30 Mon-Sat; 12-10.30 Sun

WALK 28 **Across Wimbledon Common**

WALK INFORMATION
Number of pubs: 6
Distance: 4 miles (6.4 km)
Key attractions:
Wimbledon Windmill Museum, Southside House, Canizzaro Park.
Beer range: ★
Pub architecture: ★★
Links: to walk 4

This trail is one for those who are prepared to mix drinking and walking, and takes in a stroll across Wimbledon Common, one of London's most pleasant open spaces, as well as a part of adjacent Putney Heath. On a smaller scale there is the option to visit Cannizaro Park, one of the finest of its kind, en route. It could be extended by a visit to other pubs in Wimbledon village, but you may need to conserve some energy for the walk, so I recommend sticking to the route here!

Wimbledon will be familiar to many visitors as the home of the annual tennis tournament, but it is an old settlement in its own right. However, on emerging from Wimbledon station at the start of this trail, you are greeted by a modern railway suburb. Old Wimbledon village is the best part of a mile away at the top of the hill, and that's where you want to be. I recommend that you cross the road outside the station and take the frequent no 93 bus. Alight in the village at the *Dog & Fox*, a prominent Young's pub on a left-hand bend. Opposite, under a small tower, is the **Brewery Tap 1**, the first port of call on the trail. Like most pubs carrying this name, it was built adjacent to a brewery, but the latter was burnt down in Victorian times. The pub itself has been modernised in a café-bar style, and all partitions are long gone, but the old plans can be seen on the wall. The real attraction here is the interesting range of well-kept beers. In addition to the regular ales from Adnams and Fuller's, there are two guests, which sometimes include a mild, a style of beer rarely available in London these days.

Walk through the rest of the village to the war memorial at the southern edge of Wimbledon Common. Bear left here and stroll along the edge of the Common heading westwards along Southside. In no time at all you will arrive at a small green opposite the entrance to King's College School. Look out for a small street called Crooked Billet, where there are two Young's pubs. One of these is also named the **Crooked Billet 2**, while the nearer one is the **Hand in Hand 3**. The setting is agreeable and both pubs serve Young's fine beers. Despite obvious alterations and extensions, both buildings have some character remaining, so maybe a small glass in each will enable you to come to your own opinion about their respective merits. There's an interesting story behind the name of the street. In the days when many people were illiterate and it was difficult to differentiate beerhouses from ordinary dwellings, it was common for the owner to display some sign outside the door to indicate that ale was for sale. A popular artefact was a stick, or billet, cut from any tree, hence the possible derivation here. Food is available in both pubs.

Retrace your steps as far as the road junction, then bear left into West Side Common, walking along the edge of the open space with the entrance to the excellent Cannizaro Park on your left. The grounds of Cannizaro House are perhaps the best public example of the large gardens that surrounded London mansions in the nineteenth century. There is a 'formal garden', a pool and a woodland garden, and a visit is well recommended if you have time. Continue for about half a mile as far as Camp Road on the same side, where you will almost immediately come upon the **Fox & Grapes 7**. There's enough of architectural interest in this large pub to merit it a place on CAMRA's *Regional Inventory*, although relatively little of the current buildings have survived alteration. The near end is thought to have been a stable block, probably converted between the First and Second World Wars to a rather barn-like dining hall; it sports some attractive window glass. The far end of the pub, which is likely to date from late Victorian times, has a more atmospheric bar with full-height wall panelling and a low panelled ceiling. The place has a pleasant

ambience, especially in less busy periods. The beer range includes Courage and (usually) Hog's Back T.E.A. Footy fans may like to know that the first Wimbledon football team, who played up on the Common, used the pub as their changing rooms until about 1890.

Leave the pub and continue along West Side Common past some attractive little cottages in a surprisingly rural setting, with no other trace of the built environment visible across the Common. Given its pastoral nature even now, it's no surprise to learn that this area was the haunt of highwaymen and cut-throats, as well as the scene of numerous duels many years ago. When the road turns 90° left, continue onto the Common itself along the right of two prominent forking paths, that doubles as a cycle route. Follow this through the trees for over half a mile until it merges right with an even larger track. There is a golf fairway to the left and the sails of a windmill ahead, which is reached through a gate onto a roadway. The windmill itself was built by a Roehampton carpenter two years after the Battle of Waterloo. A plaque outside tells us that Baden-Powell wrote part of *Scouting for Boys* here.

The **Fox and Grapes** Wimbledon Common

The cottage origins of the **Green Man** Putney Heath can be seen here

ROEHAMPTON

PUTNEY HEATH

HIGH ST

5

6

PUTNEY HEATH

A3

A219

Windmill

Golf Course

Path

WIMBLEDON COMMON

4

CANNIZARO PARK

WEST SIDE COMMON

SOUTHSIDE

2 **3**

HIGH ST

1

WIMBLEDON VILLAGE

WIMBLEDON HILL RD

Wimbledon

500 m

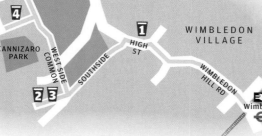

The Windmill on Wimbledon Common

From the windmill continue ahead through a second gate, past an old cattle trough adorned with the inscription of the 'Metropolitan Drinking Fountain and Cattle Trough Association'. Beyond this, take the left fork in the path at about 45°, which once again is a cycle track. Follow this path to the A3, which is less than half a mile away. Fortunately, there is a subway to save you from having to cross this gruesome road, so take it and continue to follow the cycle path as it curves left to almost join the road, then bear right past the pond. Thirty yards past the pond, fork left and after following the yellow brick road (honest!) for a few minutes you will reach a road junction, with the Roehampton war memorial in the greenery to your right. You may be ready for a beer by now and help is at hand. Continue across the road into Treville Street, which is straight ahead, and turn left at the T-junction into Roehampton High Street. Walk downhill for a few minutes and you will arrive at the **Angel** 5, a pleasantly unpretentious Young's house which retains its public bar. Food is available most hours.

Return up the High Street to the junction. If you have had enough greenery for the day, simply walk about half a mile up the road called Putney Heath, to the last pub, the Green Man. However, a more pleasant, option is to walk via the Heath, which is alongside the road. What's more, there is very little extra distance. Go back to the war memorial and continue on the same path that you arrived on, going beyond the memorial for some 30 yards. Turn left here onto a dirt track through the woods, and take the first left again. Now, fork right shortly afterwards, and this brings you, via a clearing, to a quiet

road, which you should cross by the house. Continue to the metal gate, taking the right-hand track and ignoring all side paths, until you reach a road by another gate. Follow this quiet lane down to the junction with the main road, which will take five minutes. The **Green Man** 6 is opposite the bus terminus.

A Young's pub since 1831, from the outside it still looks a bit like the rural cottage it undoubtedly once was. Although opened up, it retains some vestiges of that rural character, with several distinct areas, some of which are wood-panelled. To the rear is also a garden. A gibbet, where some of Putney Heath's many highwaymen were hanged, preceded the bus terminus. Even Dick Turpin himself was rumoured to have hidden his guns in the pub. When you are ready to go home, buses will take you to all parts of London from across the road, including Wimbledon, Clapham Junction, Wandsworth and the central area. **[LINK]**

LINK Walk 4, **Wandsworth Town** (page 21). A short bus journey, route 170, into Wandsworth will enable you to pick up the trail.

PUB INFORMATION for walk 28 **Across Wimbledon Common**

1 Brewery Tap
68-9 High Street, SW19
020 8947 9331
11-11 Mon–Sat; 12-10.30 Sun

2 Crooked Billet
15 Crooked Billet, SW19
020 8946 4942
11-11 Mon–Sat; 12-10.30 Sun

3 Hand in Hand
6 Crooked Billet, SW19
020 8946 5720
11-11 Mon–Sat; 12-10.30 Sun

4 Fox & Grapes
9 Camp Road, SW19
020 8946 5599
11-11 Mon–Sat; 12-10.30 Sun
CAMRA Regional Inventory

5 Angel
11 Roehampton High Street, SW15
020 8788 1997
11-11 Mon–Sat; 12-10.30 Sun

6 Green Man
Putney Heath, SW15
020 8788 8096
11-11 Mon–Sat; 12-10.30 Sun

A Wandsworth Common Circular

Number of pubs: 7
Distance: 3¾ miles (6 km)
Key attractions:
Wandsworth Common,
Wandsworth Nature
Study Centre,
Royal Victoria Patriotic
Building.
Beer range: ★★★
Pub architecture: ★★
Links: to walk 4

For those living north of the river who look down on South London, this may be the walk to change your mind. There is enough gentrification on this pleasant trail to please the most discriminating of urban snobs, whilst retaining a good selection of pubs that serve an honest, unpretentious pint. All in all it's a good, highly recommended trail through some attractive urban open apace and appealing residential areas. What more could you want? This is also a great walk for a summer's day.

Start at Clapham Junction, which is not, admittedly, the first place hard pressed South London commuters would associate with a serene pub walk. Leave by the main entrance into St John's Hill, head uphill to the right of the busy main road over the rail bridge, and cross straight over at the traffic lights. Thereafter, the road improves and our first trees of the day appear. It's a good five-minute walk beyond the traffic lights to your first quarry, passing upmarket specialist shops and eateries on your left. The **Beehive** ▮ is a good down-to-earth, no-frills pub where a mix of customers share a small but convivial space. Acquired by Fuller's in 1980, this pub is clean and neat, and hasn't forgotten what a local should be like. It's primarily a drinkers' pub although bar food is available.

Coming out of the Beehive, retrace your steps as far as Spencer Road, the first turning on the right. A left turn at the end of this short street brings us to the next pub, the **Freemasons** ▮. Retaining some of its former

The **Beehive**

The handsome facade of the **Freemasons**

corner site grandeur, which includes a sizeable mosaic at the entrance, this pub has nonetheless been thoroughly smartened up to an extent that would normally put off this traditionalist old bore, but I like it and so do lots of others. It has had a chequered history, having been the *Roundhouse* for many years, before undergoing two other name changes and settling on the Freemasons in 2003. High and airy, with large windows, the pub has an array of comfy seating in the modern style around the bay frontage. It's really a well regarded gastropub with some foreign beers on draught as well as real ales like Taylor Landlord and usually an Everards beer. There is room to sit outside, although it's rather noisy given its location.

On leaving, cross the main road and take Spencer Park, with the railway on one side and Wandsworth Common on the other. Shortly, you will pass the memorial to the Clapham Junction rail disaster of December 1988, in which 35 people died when three rush hour trains collided in the cutting below. Soon after that there is an isolated remnant of a smock windmill looking rather sorry for itself. This is all that remains of a project by the long vanished London & South Western Railway to pump water from this railway cutting. Just beyond the mill, turn left over the railway into a modern housing development called John Archer Way: it's ironic that this trendy little development in Tory Wandsworth is named after a veteran of the Trotskyite movement. Almost straightaway you are face to face with a huge Victorian Gothic pile, which despite its size is surprisingly well hidden and in here is your next pub. It was originally built as an asylum and then later became a school, hospital, and during the Second World War was used by MI5 and MI6. Nazi supremo Rudolf Hess was apparently detained in the cellar dungeon. However, in the early 1980s it was considered beyond repair when acquired by the present owner for £1. After being totally destroyed by

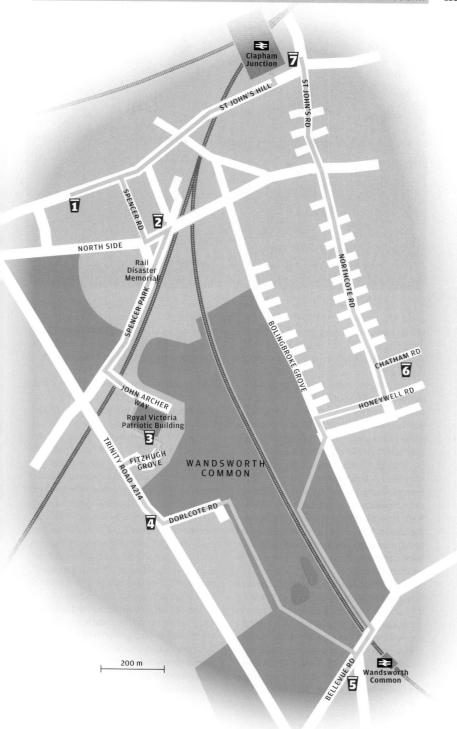

Clapham
Junction 7

ST JOHN'S HILL

ST JOHN'S RD

1

SPENCER RD

2

NORTH SIDE

Rail
Disaster
Memorial

SPENCER PARK

NORTHCOTE RD

BOLINGBROKE GROVE

CHATHAM RD
6

JOHN ARCHER
WAY

Royal Victoria
Patriotic Building
3

HONEYWELL RD

FITZHUGH
GROVE

TRINITY ROAD A214

WANDSWORTH
COMMON

4

DORLCOTE RD

200 m

BELLEVUE RD

Wandsworth
Common
5

Asylum, school, hospital, wartime hideout, ruin, and now home

arson, the magnificent hall with its painted ceiling was carefully reconstructed, and deservedly won a Civic Trust Award as well as the prized Europa Nostra Order of Merit. Now the building houses a dance and drama school, flats and studios, workshops and **Le Gothique** 🗿 restaurant and bar, one of London's first gastropubs. It is closed on Sundays and usually used for private parties on Saturdays, so it's well worth ringing ahead to check. If you do visit, the attractive bar hosts beers from Ballards, Young's and Shepherd Neame. To find it, go round the front of the building or back to the diametrically opposite corner, through an archway. If you are doing the trail during the week and have time to linger, this would make a good lunch stop: the garden eatery in the Victorian cloisters is considered by some to be London's finest.

Leaving Le Gothique, exit under the archway and follow the quiet Fitzhugh Grove as it twists left and right before emerging onto the busy dual carriageway of Trinity Road. If Le Gothique is closed and you don't want to detour through its grounds, simply continue straight ahead past the windmill and turn left into Trinity Road. Turn left again to keep the Common on your left, and the next pub

can be seen not too far off on the other side of the road. This is the **County Arms** 🗿, which was once a contender for the CAMRA *Regional Inventory* but was then controversially refurbished. That said, I have to admit that the place doesn't look at all bad. This is a Young's tied house, and financially it certainly justifies the large sum that they must have spent to make this big place appeal to the well-heeled locals. Bits of the old pub remain, such as a mosaic, vestiges of screenwork with some very nice etched glass, splendid fireplaces and decent woodwork, which are complemented with lots of modern seats, chunky kitsch tables and a very swanky eating area towards the rear. Beyond this is a large and secluded garden area, kitted out, appropriately for the area, with lots of trendy decking. Although the pub probably sells more Pimms and wine than bitter, there is nothing wrong with the beer quality. Judge for yourselves.

Time to explore Wandsworth Common, which you have skated around so far. Cross the road again and head off at 90° down Dorlcote Road to join the Common. Turn right on to a cinder track, and follow this to an attractive pond with some enticing seats if you want to rest awhile. Keep pretty much on the same bearing, which has now become a paved path, emerging very shortly onto the busy road close to the railway bridge. The imposing bulk of the **Hope** 5 is on the corner. This is another pub that has had a serious makeover, leaving it with a bistro/wine bar atmosphere. However, the real pull here is the beer, which is a changing range of unusual ales, many coming from microbreweries, plus several interesting foreign beers. It's a popular place and can get rather full. There is also seating outside, which, although it is constrained by the roads on either side, is not unpleasant on a sunny day. There are some of those very popular George Bush-approved 'global warming' heaters too for when it's really a bit cold for sipping Pimms *à l'exterieur*.

If by now you have had enough, Wandsworth Common station is just across the road; otherwise, cross the road and the rail bridge on the right, then turn sharp left onto a path alongside the tracks to your left with Common on your right. A pleasant, leisurely ten-minute stroll brings you to a point where a rail footbridge comes in from the left. Take the diagonal path at 45° right across the Common to join the road close to a set of traffic lights. If you prefer to meander across the Common rather than hold to the path, simply look for these traffic lights and the main road, Bolingbroke Grove, when you reach the other side. Take the right turning beyond the lights into Honeywell Road, then turn left at Northcote Road, and first right again into Chatham Road. Halfway up here, on the right, you'll find the **Eagle Ale House** 6. Comfortable seating, nice woodwork and even the traces of its former compartmented layout await you in this side street local, which has a relaxing ambience and reliable beers. These usually include Fuller's London Pride, Timothy Taylor Landlord and a guest from Enterprise Inns' list. There is also a small

The 'Mightily impressive' **Falcon**

The curved bar in the **Falcon** is thought to be the longest continuous bar counter in the country

courtyard to the rear with a marquee. This is a good spot to lounge around over a beer or two before setting off for your last port of call on this enjoyable but punishing itinerary around South London.

Drop back down to the Northcote Road and turn right along this busy but lively and interesting road, which is lined with unusual and upmarket shops as you approach Clapham Junction. At the traffic lights cross straight over into St John's Road, and at the far end, as you emerge back at Clapham Junction, the imposing **Falcon** 7 stands on the corner of the crossroads. Aptly described in CAMRA's *London Regional Inventory* as 'mightily impressive', this late Victorian pub can be viewed to good effect from across the street. Inside, what some say is the longest

continuous bar counter in the country curves around a spacious servery. A real impression of height prevails in the bar back and the windows. Some fine screenwork survives as well, as does a charming stained glass window depicting the eponymous bird of prey. Given that this pub is so well known, being almost right outside the station, don't expect the place to yourself. It can get very busy and noisy especially in the evenings. Nonetheless it's certainly worth a visit. Beers are usually from Adnams and Fuller's: food is available at lunchtimes and snacks later. Clapham Junction station is a few yards along on the right upon exit from the pub.   [LINK]

LINK Walk 4, Wandsworth Town (*page 21*).
It's only one stop on the train from platforms 5/6 to the *Alma* outside the station.

PUB INFORMATION for walk 29 **A Wandsworth Common Circular**

1 Beehive
197 St. John's Hill, SW11
020 7564 1897
11–11 Mon–Sat
12–10.30 Sun

2 Freemasons
2 North Side,
Wandsworth Common, SW18
020 7326 8580
12–11 Mon–Sat
12–10.30 Sun

3 Le Gothique
The Royal Victoria Patriotic
Building, Fitzhugh Grove,
Trinity Road, SW18
020 8870 6567
11am–midnight Mon–Fri
Usually closed Saturdays
Closed Sundays

4 County Arms
345 Trinity Road, SW18
020 8874 8532
11–11 Mon–Thurs
11am–midnight Fri
12–midnight Sat; 12–10.30 Sun

5 Hope
1 Bellevue Road, SW17
020 8672 8717
11am–11.30pm Mon–Sat
12–10.30 Sun

6 Eagle Ale House
104 Chatham Road, SW11
020 7228 2328
12–11 Mon–Sat; 12–10.30 Sun

7 Falcon
2 St John's Hill, SW11
020 7924 8040
11–11 Mon–Sat; 12–10.30 Sun
CAMRA National Inventory

Hampstead and Highgate

WALK INFORMATION
Number of pubs: 7
Distance: 2⅜ miles (3.75 km)
Key attractions: Freud Museum, Kenwood House, Highgate village & cemetery.
Beer range: ★★
Pub architecture: ★★★
Links: to walk 3

To finish the book, this is an all-purpose trail between two of London's prettiest suburbs, which takes in one of the capital's largest and most celebrated open spaces. You can choose to do just the Hampstead part or the Highgate section of this walk. Alternatively you can walk between the two, which is highly recommended, or cheat and get a bus! This is a popular area and best appreciated on a weekday, starting early in Hampstead, enjoying a siesta on the Heath and finishing up in Highate mid to late afternoon. The famous Highgate cemetery, Karl Marx's burial place, is in Swain's Lane, close to the Highgate Flask.

Start at Hampstead underground station, the deepest on the whole London system. Note the attractive ticket windows at the exit. Here, there is also a detailed map listing most Hampstead pubs on a larger scale than the one in this book. Hampstead developed from a fashionable spa in the eighteenth century and although its days as a spa were quite short-lived, the height of the area encouraged the wealthy to move in, while its steepness discouraged the worst sort of Victorian property speculation. This means that the Georgian character of the old village has survived despite the very apparent affluence here.

The place to head for first is very close. Turn right out of the station down the street and Flask Walk is a few yards on your left. Down this atmospheric passage is a great Hampstead institution, the **Flask Tavern** 🍺. Formerly serving a relatively working class district, where the houses now fetch astro-

nomical sums, the Flask's name derives from the wells associated with the aforementioned spa: these pure waters were bottled and sold at threepence a flask in the *Thatched House*, a forerunner of this pub on the same site. Originally known as the *Lower Flask* since there was another on East Heath Road, the present building dates back to 1874; it has been a Young's house since 1904, so expect their beers. Inside, it retains two bars, divided by a large screen. The 'Public' bar on the left was formerly further divided – note the old 'Private Bar' sign on the disused door to the side. Despite there being two small TVs on display, the pub has thankfully shed the large TV screen of its 'sports bar' incarnation of a few years ago. The linoleum is still there, as is a tiled dado rail, and despite the creeping gentrification it's still a good room to drink in. The larger saloon with its bare floorboards leads to an eatery at the rear.

Moving on, go back to the underground station, and cross over the main road onto Holly Hill, opposite. Not far up here is a welcoming pub sign, still bearing the old Benskins livery, of a another venerable Hampstead institution, the **Holly Bush 2**. The pub itself is just off to the right. Having survived an attempt by its former owners to wreck it in the late 1990s, it looks set to enjoy a great future. It has to be one of my favourite London pubs simply on account of the building – a splendidly anarchic huddle of rooms, snugs and corridors, although purists will point out that it has nonetheless been considerably altered, with much of the rear area having been brought into pub use from private quarters. It is immensely enjoyable for all that, and the delightful shabbiness simply adds to the atmosphere. Despite, or more likely *on account* of it being Hampstead, the place hasn't been tarted up beyond recognition like other pubs you could mention. Etched glass conveys the former function of separate rooms, like the 'Coffee Room' which still has an open fire. Beers are from Adnams, Fuller's and, unusually for north of the Thames, Harveys.

An old Benskins Brewery sign in Hampstead

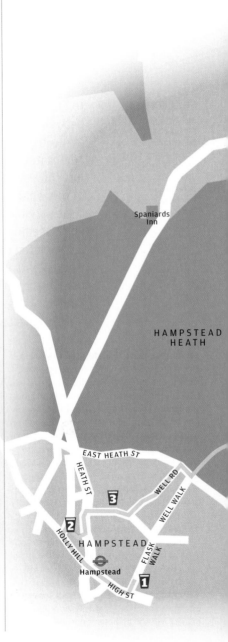

Spaniards Inn

HAMPSTEAD HEATH

EAST HEATH ST

HEATH ST

WELL RD

WELL WALK

3

2

HOLLY HILL

HAMPSTEAD

FLASK WALK

Hampstead

1

HIGH ST

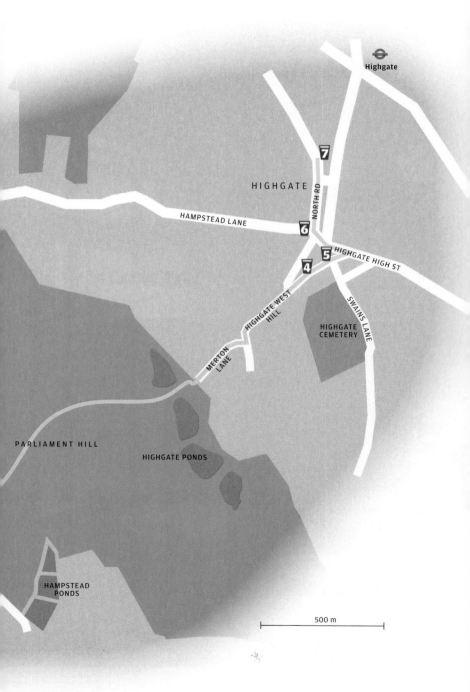

Highgate

HIGHGATE

HAMPSTEAD LANE

NORTH RD

7

6

5 HIGHGATE HIGH ST

4

HIGHGATE WEST HILL

MERTON LANE

SWAINS LANE

HIGHGATE CEMETERY

PARLIAMENT HILL

HIGHGATE PONDS

HAMPSTEAD PONDS

500 m

Inside the **Holly Bush** Hampstead

An old fireplace in the **Holly Bush**

The streets around the Holly Bush on the Mount are probably the most attractive part of Hampstead, and repay a stroll. The easiest way to find your next pub is to return down the hill to the main road and follow it north past the *Horse & Groom*, known by some as the *Remorse & Gloom*, and turn right into New End, a couple of hundred yards beyond. Down here you will meet the **Duke of Hamilton** ③ sitting above the street on the left. For devotees of architecture, especially those bowled over by the Holly Bush, the interior is pretty plain and the window police ought to pay a visit! Nevertheless, the welcome is warm, and there is no other pub in Hampstead that has a better record of serving consistently good ale as local CAMRA awards for Pub of the Year testify to this. Fuller's beers are sold, and moreover the Duke remains a community local that hasn't been subject to gastrophication and for that we should be grateful.

As we leave the Duke it's decision time. If you are continuing over the Heath to Highgate then ignore the next section. If not, obviously returning back to the top of the hill and turning left will bring you to central Hampstead again. However, if you are game for another pub or two, try either the *Old White Bear* just down the hill from the Duke, where there is a decent selection of beers in a pub with some history, or visit the *Three Horseshoes* back in central Hampstead on Heath Street just yards beyond the underground station. This is a former Wetherspoon's with a good beer range.

Bus to Highgate

For those moving on to Highgate from the Duke, if you want to bus it, the stop for the 603 (weekdays only until about 3pm) is up on Heath Street. If it's a weekend you will have to walk up to the junction with Heath Street and North End Way to pick up the 210. If using the bus option you could always alight at the historic *Spaniards Inn*, which lies on the route, and continue on a later bus. On arrival at Highgate, the bus stop in the High Street is very close to the Prince of Wales, which we will be visiting soon. For now, take the road (South Grove) past the bus terminal and in no time you will encounter the Flask (see below).

Walking to Highgate

The walk across the Heath to Highgate is the longest refreshment-free walk in the book, with about two miles separating the Duke of Hamilton at Hampstead and the Flask at Highgate. To start, come out of the Duke of Hamilton, turn left and walk down to the *White Bear*, then turn left again along the frontage of the pub into Wells Road, following it to the point where it meets the busy East Heath Road at the edge of the Heath. Cross this road carefully and walk 30 yards downhill to the point where a wide gravelly track descends on to the Heath alongside a group of tall flats. Now, it's simplicity itself to follow this wide path for some time as it makes its way to Highgate ponds; look out for the views across to the church at Highgate at one point. At the pond, the path turns to tarmac. Follow the wider path here as it climbs the short distance uphill to gain the roadway by the water fountain and toilets. Take the road straight across and follow this until it reaches a far busier road a few minutes later. Follow this one to the left and up the steep hill to reach the **Flask** ④ by a fork in the road. Note that you will see the sign before the pub.

The Flask is an old pub which has been significantly altered over the years. Although it retains some character as befits a venerable old building, its refurbishment seems to have taken away its soul. There are, however, still several separate areas, and the old bar servery survives but is no longer used. The garden/patio outside is agreeable enough if not too busy, but the place gets packed at times and to arrive when it's quiet is quite an achievement. The beer quality is high enough to earn the pub a place in the *Good Beer Guide*, however, and the range is good with Adnams Broadside and Timothy Taylor's Landlord being served alongside up to four regularly changing guest beers.

Now from the Flask's front door bear left, and follow South Grove past the bus terminal and you will see the rear of your next pub, the **Prince of Wales** 5, almost immediately. Follow the High Street up to enter the pub, which is a handsome brick building on Highgate's main street, with several distinct but interconnected drinking and eating areas around a central servery. Three real ales from Young's, Marston's and Theakston's are served in the sort of place where people still sit around reading the paper and maybe planning the overthrow of capitalism.

Don't get too comfortable here, for you still have two pubs to visit. Just a stone's throw up the road, at the junction with Highgate School opposite, sits a very significant Highgate landmark, **The Gatehouse** 6. The name refers to a former tollgate and archway over the road, which was the former boundary between Middlesex and London. The earliest mention of The Gatehouse in licensing records is around 1670, and amongst the former glitterati who have been here were Byron, Dickens and Cruickshank. However, the mock Tudor style of the pub we see today only goes back to the early twentieth century. The upstairs of the pub was previously used as a courtroom, but now it's a very successful fringe theatre, and to top it all there is a resident lady ghost! As the pub is now part of the Wetherspoon's empire you can expect the company stamp on the décor and fittings, with the normal good range of beers, and long food hours.

After this, walk along North Road to the north of the pub, opposite the school. Check your watch and the opening times in the panel here, and hopefully you can set off for the last pub, the **Wrestlers** 7. Considered by many to be the finest pub in Highgate Village, it has stood on this site since 1547, although the current building dates to 1921. The star of the show in the atmospheric interior with its dark panelling is the impressive fireplace, which evidently survived the 1920s refurbishment. You can learn for yourself about the curious ancient ceremony of 'swearing on the horns', for the horns in question, and the procedure, are there above the fireplace.

By now you will be ready for a train home. Simply turn down the alley immediately to the side of the pub, and on reaching the road at the bottom turn sharp left and walk the short distance to the Archway Road. Highgate underground station on the Northern Line is just to your right.   [LINK]

LINK Walk 3, Kentish Town (*page 17*). A 214 bus from Highgate, or two stops on the Underground from Archway, will deliver you right opposite the Assembly House and the start of the trail.

PUB INFORMATION for walk 30 **Hampstead and Highgate**

1 Flask Tavern (Hampstead)
14 Flask Walk, Hampstead, NW3
020 7435 4580:
11–11 Mon–Sat; 12–10.30 Sun
CAMRA Regional Inventory

2 Holly Bush
22 Holly Mount, Hampstead, NW3
020 7435 2892
12–11 Mon–Sat; 12–10.30 Sun
CAMRA Regional Inventory

3 Duke of Hamilton
23 New End, Hampstead, NW3
020 7794 0258
12–11 Mon–Sat; 12–10.30 Sun

4 Flask (Highgate)
77 Highgate West Hill, N6
020 8348 7346
11–11 Mon–Sat;
Noon–10.30pm Sun
CAMRA Regional Inventory

5 Prince of Wales
53 Highgate High Street, N6
020 8340 0445
11–11 Mon–Sat; 12–10.30 Sun

6 The Gatehouse
1 North Road, Highgate, N6
020 8340 8054
10am–11pm Mon–Sat
10am–10.30pm Sun

7 Wrestlers
98 North Road, Highgate, N6
020 8340 4297
4.30pm–11pm Mon–Fri
12–11 Sat; 12–10.30 Sun

Beer styles

Porter and Stout

Porter originated as a London beer, a blend of brown ale, pale ale and 'stale' or well-matured ale. It acquired the name Porter as a result of its popularity among London's street-market workers. The strongest versions of Porter were known as Stout Porter, reduced over the years to simply Stout. Today we associate the style with Ireland of course, mainly down to Dublin brewer Arthur Guinness who imitated the style and added his own dry roast twist. Restrictions on making roasted malts in Britain during World War One left the market open to the Irish. In recent years, smaller craft brewers in Britain have rekindled an interest in both Porters and Stouts, although it is relatively rare to find it in London pubs owing to the shortage of genuine free houses offering microbrewery beers. Your best chance is the JD Wetherspoon chain where there is often a good range of guest beers, or the Porterhouse in Covent Garden, although even their Stouts and Porters are pasteurised. Look for profound dark and roasted malt character with fruit, coffee, liquorice and/or molasses, all underscored by hop bitterness.

IPA and Pale Ale

The new technologies of the Industrial Revolution enabled brewers to use pale malts to fashion beers that were genuinely golden or pale bronze in colour. First brewed in London and Burton-on-Trent for the colonial market, IPAs were strong in alcohol and high in hops: the preservative character of the hops helped keep the beers in good condition during long sea journeys. Modern so-called IPAs with strengths of around 3.5%, like the widely available Greene King IPA, are not strictly-speaking IPAs, with the real thing starting at 5.5% and moving onwards and upwards. London Greenwich brewers Meantime have produced a scorchingly hoppy and historically accurate bottle-conditioned IPA, as have Hoxton microbrewery Pitfield. On the flavour front look for good malt character, tangy citrus fruitiness and a big spicy, bitter hop character which lingers.

Pale Ales were late-Victorian younger cousins of IPA, still gold in colour, though lower in alcohol and not as hoppy. They were developed for the domestic market during the Victorian period and usually bottled. Today a real Pale Ale is a rare beast, with Marston's Pedigree still remaining a shining example of this style (providing you can get it served in good condition).

Bitter

This is probably the most common style of cask ale available in London, but it was not always so. From the end of the nineteenth century, brewers acquired large estates of pubs in London, and moved away from vatted beers such as Porter that were stored for many months. They developed 'running beers' that could be served after a few days' storage in pub cellars. Bitter grew out of Pale Ale and is similar in style, most falling into the 3.4% to 3.9% band, with more full-bodied Best Bitters being 4% upwards. Young's Bitter, from one of the capital's old established family brewers, is an excellent example, and another, now widely available, is Adnams Bitter from Suffolk.

Extra or Special Strong Bitters of 5% or more include Fuller's ESB and Greene King Abbot, both widely available in London. With ordinary Bitter, look for plenty of hop character, a powerful bitterness, maybe with tangy fruit and/or nutty malt characteristics. Stronger bitters tend to be maltier and fruitier but hop aroma and bitterness are still crucial to the style, and are often achieved by 'late hopping'.

Golden Ales

This new style of winsomely gold, well-hopped and quenching beer was developed in the 1980s as independent brewers attempted to win younger drinkers over from heavily-promoted lager brands. Exmoor Gold was the first, though Hop Back's Summer Lightning became the most well-known. Strengths range from 3.5% to 5%. The hallmark is the biscuity and juicy malt character derived from pale malts, underscored by tart citrus fruit and in some, the use of aromatic hops. Above all, such beers are quenching and are served cool. Good exam-

ples found in the capital are Discovery from Fuller's, and Deuchars IPA, brewed in Edinburgh but widely available as a guest beer.

Mild

Mild was once the most popular style of beer but was overtaken by Bitter from the 1950s. It was developed in the eighteenth and nineteenth centuries as a less aggressively bitter style of beer than porter and stout, though recent research suggests it got its name from the fact that it was a young (mild) beer as opposed to the long-slumbering vatted Porters. Mild ale is usually dark brown in colour due to the use of well-roasted malts or roasted barley. It is only very rarely spotted in London pubs.

Based on Roger Protz's Beer Styles feature for the *Good Beer Guide* 2006 (CAMRA Books)

Historic pub interiors

The pub is one of the great British traditions, stretching back into antiquity and reinforced by pub signs such as 'Ye Olde...' etc. Ironically, despite such appeals to tradition and history, precious few pub interiors have much claim to antiquity, and this is as true in London as anywhere else in Britain. Very few of the capital's pubs have survived the last fifty years without significant alteration.

Defending Britain's traditional pubs, as well as its traditional beers, has always been one of CAMRA's declared concerns. By the early 1980s, when the Campaign set up its Pub Preservation Group, it had become apparent that the nation's pub heritage was being largely ignored by mainstream conservation bodies. Change in pubs has always occurred, and has reflected developments in society; but since the 1960s and 1970s in particular, the British pub has been subject to an accelerated and often destructive wave of internal alterations. A major component of that change has been the opening up of pubs, the removal of screens and partitions, (many of which contained very fine work) and the installation of new, often very inferior, fittings. This process has been particularly destructive in London, since the Victorian passion for private drinking spaces went further in the capital city than elsewhere.

The relationship to statutory listing

Some readers will be aware that in the United Kingdom many buildings are statutorily 'listed'. This means they meet strict national criteria of 'architectural or historic interest'. The weakness of the listing process is that it has always concentrated primarily upon the exterior fabric, often with little reference to the internal fittings. Not surprisingly, there-fore, statutory listing in itself has failed to save many priceless pub interiors. Moreover, many of our most unspoilt pubs have no architectural pretensions at all – the simple rural beerhouse and the plain urban public bar, which have been the biggest casualties in the relentless 'modernisation' process, remain unprotected by listing.

CAMRA's Inventory of Historic Pub Interiors

CAMRA's concern about the fate of authentic historic pub interiors met with strong support from English Heritage, and the CAMRA National Inventory, (NI) referred to throughout this guide, was born. It identifies pubs that retain the most complete and important historic interiors in the country. Its sole concern is with the internal physical fabric of those pubs, in terms of historical intactness – and rarity value. As a result of this project, several plain and simple pubs, like the Hand & Shears, EC1, and the Wheatsheaf, SE1, commonplace thirty years ago but now very rare, enjoy listed status.

The **Hand & Shears**

The project also highlighted the extreme rarity of intact inter-war pubs, like the Hope & Anchor in Hammersmith, of which there are very few in London. Ironically the showy and glamorous pubs from the 1890s, the golden age of London pub-building, have survived rather better.

The National Inventory represents the very best of our pub heritage, but there are many other pubs, which although altered, still retain enough of historic interest to be regarded as of regional significance. The CAMRA London Pubs Group, established in 1992, set about the task of identifying other important historic pub interiors throughout the capital that included a significant amount of genuinely historic internal fabric and/or sufficient of

its original layout for the historic plan-form to be appreciated and understood. CAMRA's Regional Inventory for London was published in 2004 and many of the pubs therein are included on walks in this guide. Examples included are the Ten Bells, Spitalfields, E1, where the pub has been gutted but its splendid tiling survives, and the Pineapple, Kentish Town, NW5, with its particularly notable early bar back.

Encouragingly, there are signs that the very best historic pub interiors are starting to be valued and marketed for what they are – the Black Friar, EC4, and the Salisbury, WC2, are cases in point. We hope that this, CAMRA's first book of London pub walks, will be part of that process of awareness raising.

Clockwise from top left: the **Salisbury**, the **Hope & Anchor**, the **Black Friar** (*exterior and interior*) and the **Ten Bells**

A word about pub etiquette – a guide for overseas visitors

British pubs are famous all over the world, but if you have rarely or never been in one before, it might be worth knowing a few things about the British way of going about getting your drinks, which may well be different where you come from...

How do you order?

In some ways this is relatively easy. You decide what you want to drink, go up to the bar counter and tell the serving staff what you want: they will bring it to you at the counter, tell you how much it costs, you pay for it and that's it ... job done! You can then either take your drinks to a table or remain standing at the bar. This one-stage process is quite different from the Continental method which is: sit down, wait, order (if a waiter appears), wait, drinks appear, wait for bill, wait for change ... maybe leave a tip. Receipts are not usual in Britain, but in larger and more modern pubs you can normally get one if you ask.

What to drink?

Having bought this book, you will, we hope, be keen to try traditional British draught beer, although there are plenty of other options including soft drinks. However, simply asking for 'a beer' won't do, since most of the pubs in this book will have a variety of them. It is much more usual in Britain to ask for a beer by name – most real ales are identified by a handpump on which there is a clip carrying the name of the beer. Draught beer is normally served in one pint (568ml) measures but you can also order it in half pints. Contrary to malicious rumours, we Brits *don't* drink 'warm' beer: traditional beer should be served at about 12-14 degrees C (54-57 F).

Tipping

Tips are *not* usual in pubs and are not expected. Occasionally people say 'have one on me' (the price of a small drink) or 'keep the change'. But that sort of thing usually only happens if the order is a big one or the bar person has been particularly helpful.

Cash or credit cards?

Normally, payment is made in cash, though some larger pubs may take credit cards for orders over £5, (ask first if you want to take this option).

Traditional beer

The section on beer styles (p. 145) may be useful reading here. Unlike lager, there are many different flavours and traditional beer, or real ale as it is also known, comes in various strengths ranging from about 3.6% to over 5% alcohol by volume.

Pub food

Pubs have long been popular places to eat. They are less formal than restaurants and are usually cheaper. You generally order at the bar and, again, tipping is not expected. The range of food varies enormously from pub to pub. The popular phrase 'bar food' (often seen outside pubs) can mean almost anything, but typically refers to things like steak, omelettes, lasagne, steak and kidney pie, and salads, often all served with chips (French fries). Common terms that might be confusing are 'Ploughman's' and 'Jackets'. The former means bread and usually salad and pickles, served with cheese or sometimes ham or paté: the latter refers to potatoes baked in their skins and served with a variety of fillings like cheese, baked beans, or tuna. Many pubs serve the traditional British Sunday lunch of roast meat with potatoes and vegetables.

A recent trend has been the arrival of the 'gastropub' – a halfway house between a pub and a restaurant, where the emphasis is on good food, often using local and seasonal produce, rather than on alcoholic beverages. In general, pub food is often pretty good and sometimes excellent.

Naming the rooms

The traditional British pub used to have two or more rooms. You can still often see notices on doors or lettering in glass panels saying (to name the most frequent) 'Public Bar', 'Private Bar', 'Saloon', and 'Lounge'. These are reminders of the days when the Public Bar was the least prestigious room and the Private Bar a more intimate place for regulars. The other rooms were 'better class' spaces where drinks cost a small amount more. Beginning in the 1960s, there was a major move to amalgamate rooms and large numbers of pubs began to look like one another. Those that have kept the traditional separate rooms have a distinctly different and warmer atmosphere. Quite a number of them are celebrated in this guide and they are well worth seeking out.

Smoking

There has been great pressure to ban smoking in public places and it will be illegal in all pubs in Scotland from March 2006, and probably in Wales and Northern Ireland from 2007. In England our government has decided (against public opinion) to ban smoking from pubs that serve food, but not from pubs that don't, though a firm date has not yet been set for this change.

CAMRA have proposed a more sensible option which would have supported the traditional, multi-room pub – to set aside a separate room for smokers.

Pub hours

In recent years, British licensing laws have become much more liberal but all pubs have certain permitted opening hours. They usually open at 11.00am or 12.00 noon and most in this guide then stay open all day (but beware early and Sunday closing in the City). As from November 2005 many pubs have been allowed to stay open later than the traditional weekday closing time of 11.00pm, and you will find 'last orders' called at various different times. Before closing time the staff may shout 'last orders', flash the lights on and off or even ring a bell, but they may not, so keep an eye on your watch!

The 'round'

This term refers to buying a 'round of drinks' for yourself and others. If you bought the first drinks for your group, when it comes to buying some more one of your companions will say (or you hope they'll say!), 'it's my round'.

Cheers!

What do you say to your drinking companions as you are about to have a drink? The British drinking culture and vocabulary is poor in this respect. Usually we say nothing and just get on with it! 'Good health' is rather old-fashioned and rarely used. Raising the glass and saying 'cheers' is about the best we can manage!

Enjoy your pub visiting. Cheers!

GEOFF BRANDWOOD

Index of pubs

Index of beers

CAMPAIGN
FOR
REAL ALE

Books for Beer lovers

CAMRA Books, the publishing arm of the Campaign for Real Ale, is the leading publisher of books on beer and pubs. Key titles include:

Good Beer Guide 2006
Editor: **ROGER PROTZ**

The Good Beer Guide is the only guide you will need to find the right pint, in the right place, every time. It's the original and the best independent guide to around 4,500 pubs throughout the UK; the Sun newspaper rated the 2004 edition in the top 20 books of all time! Now in its 34th year, this annual publication is a comprehensive and informative guide to the best real ale pubs in the UK, researched and written exclusively by CAMRA members and fully updated every year.

£13.99   ISBN 1 85249 211 2

300 Beers to Try Before You Die
ROGER PROTZ

300 beers from around the world, handpicked by award-winning journalist, author and broadcaster Roger Protz to try before you die! A comprehensive portfolio of top beers from the smallest microbreweries in the United States to family-run British breweries and the world's largest brands. This book is indispensable for both beer novices and aficionados.

£12.99   ISBN 1 85249 213 9

The Big Book of Beer
Everything you Need to Know about the World's Greatest Drink
ADRIAN TIERNEY-JONES

Everything you could ever want to know about the world's favourite drink; this beautifully illustrated book is an eye-opener to the world of beer articulated by well-known beer experts and those who brew it. A perfect gift for the 'real beer' connoisseur.

£14.99   ISBN 1 85249 212 0

Good Beer Guide Belgium
Editor: **TIM WEBB**

Now in its 5th edition and in full colour, this book has developed a cult following among committed beer lovers and beer tourists. It is the definitive, totally independent guide to understanding and finding the best of Belgian beer and an essential companion for any beer drinker visiting Belgium or seeking out Belgian beer in Britain. Includes details of the 120 breweries and over 800 beers in regular production, as well as 500 of the best hand-picked cafes in Belgium.

£12.99   ISBN 1 85249 210 4

Good Beer Guide Germany
STEVE THOMAS

The first ever comprehensive region-by-region guide to Germany's brewers, beer and outlets. Includes more than 1,200 breweries, 1,000 brewery taps and 7,200 beers. Complete with useful travel information on how to get there, informative essays on German beer and brewing plus beer festival listings. To be published in May 2006.

£14.99   ISBN 1 85249 219 8

Good Pub Food
SUSAN NOWAK & JILL ADAM

This fully revised sixth edition of Good Pub Food singles out over 600 real ale pubs in England, Wales, Scotland and Northern Ireland, which also specialise in fine cuisine. All are highlighted on easy to use maps and have a full description of their location, ales, menus, price, vegetarian selections and facilities. Both Susan Nowak and Jill Adam have been involved in editing and compiling CAMRA guides for over 20 years. Published March 2006.

£13.99   ISBN 1 85249 214 7

CAMRA'S Good Cider Guide

The 5th edition of this title features more than 600 traditional cider producers and outlets in the UK and is an essential volume for anyone wishing to become a cider connoisseur. CAMRA'S Good Cider Guide, revised and updated, offers a county-by-county directory of UK cider producers and outlets and provides unique, in-depth knowledge for the discerning cider consumer.

£10.99   ISBN 1 85249 195 7